TRANG

The More You Give

Professor TRANG THOMAS AM

PETER NOLAN

TheBookStudio

All correspondence to the author:

Email: pierrecoolum@gmail.com

PO Box 264
Coolum Beach
Queensland 4573

© Copyright Peter Nolan

First Printed 2019

The right of Peter Nolan to be identified as the author of this work has been asserted by him in accordance with the Copyright, Designs and Patents act.

All rights reserved. No part of this publication may be reproduced, stored in or introduced into a retrieval system, or transmitted, in any form, or by any means (electronic, mechanical, photocopying, recording or otherwise) without the prior written permission of the publisher. Any person who does any unauthorised act in relation to this publication may be liable to criminal prosecution and civil claims for damages.

This book is sold subject to the condition that it shall not, by way of trade or otherwise, be lent, re-sold, hired out, or otherwise circulated without the publisher's prior consent in any form of binding or cover other than that in which it is published and without a similar condition including this condition being imposed on the subsequent purchaser.

ISBN: 978-0-6483017-0-7

Proudly produced by

TheBookStudio

www.thebookstudio.com.au

Dedication

*To Trang and her family,
in memory of their beloved husband and father, David.*

- About the Author -

Peter Nolan was born In Queensland during World War II. He is married to Robyn, a clinical psychologist. They have two sons, Michael and Brett.

After joining the RAAF at age 17, Peter spent the early to mid-1960s in Southeast Asia (Malaysia and Thailand) before serving with the Australian Army's 161 Reconnaissance Flight in Vietnam during 1967-68. He was commissioned into the Engineer Branch of the RAAF in 1970, continuing his career progress in operational, engineering and project appointments throughout Australia. From 1978 until 1982 he served on the Defence Staff at the Australian Embassy in Washington, D.C.

Following his military career, Peter completed a BA (Modern Asian Studies) at Griffith University in 1985 before serving in the Australian Public Service from 1986 to 1998. He then managed Robyn's clinical psychology practice at Coolum Beach on Queensland's Sunshine Coast. In 2002, they adopted Mingma, a teenage Sherpa girl from the Mt Everest region. Mingma completed secondary and tertiary studies to become a secondary school teacher in 2010.

Peter's keen interest in the politics, economics and history of Australia's interaction with Southeast Asia led to the publication of his first non-fiction work: *Possums and Bird Dogs*. This work, the history of Australian Army Aviation operations in South Vietnam (1965-72), filled a substantial gap in Australia's Vietnam War history and was well-received.

Peter has travelled widely and pursued community interests during his retirement. He served on the committee of the Sunshine Coast Literary Association for several years, contributing to workshops for aspiring writers. In 2013, after meeting Professor Trang Thomas in North Vietnam, he commenced researching and writing her biography.

Possums & Bird Dogs:
Australian Army Aviation's 161 Reconnaissance Flight in South Vietnam
Allen & Unwin 2006.
ISBN 1 74114 635 6 (pbk)
ISBN 1 74175 042 3 (Limited Edition HB)

– CONTENTS –

Foreword by Sir James Gobbo AC		vii
Preface		ix
Chapter 1	We Are All Australians Now	1
Chapter 2	Origins	5
Chapter 3	Childhood Memories	11
Chapter 4	Flight from Hanoi	15
Chapter 5	Saigon	19
Chapter 6	Place where the Sun Rises	27
Chapter 7	Induction	31
Chapter 8	First-Year Studies	35
Chapter 9	Second Year: Choices and Adaptation	43
Chapter 10	Third Year Studies	49
Chapter 11	Trapped in Saigon	53
Chapter 12	Honours Year	57
Chapter 13	Marriage	61
Chapter 14	Postgraduate Studies	69
Chapter 15	First Taste of Travel	73
Chapter 16	Discrimination	79
Chapter 17	Fresh Start	83
Chapter 18	First Child, First Home	89
Chapter 19	Saigon Falls	93
Chapter 20	Tragedy at Sea	97
Chapter 21	Consolidation and Crisis	101
Chapter 22	Escape from Saigon	107
Chapter 23	Trang's Thesis	133
Chapter 24	New Times, New Goals	119
Chapter 25	Doctor Trang	125

Chapter 26	Political Engagement	133
Chapter 27	Victorian Multicultural Commission	139
Chapter 28	Trang Goes International	145
Chapter 29	The Prime Minister Calls	151
Chapter 30	Trang and the Special Broadcasting Service	159
Chapter 31	Constitutional Convention	163
Chapter 32	Return to Academia	167
Chapter 33	Feminism and Recognition	173
Chapter 34	New Century, New Challenges	179
Chapter 35	Human Rights and Refugee Children	185
Chapter 36	Director of Science, Australian Psychological Society	189
Chapter 37	Driving Cross-cultural Initiatives	195
Chapter 38	Sailing before the Wind	199
Chapter 39	Retirement from RMIT University	207
Chapter 40	Fateful Diagnosis	213
Chapter 41	Troubled Times	217
Chapter 42	Vale David	221
Chapter 43	Widow Trang	225
Chapter 44	Recognition, Reprieve and Continuing Challenge	231

Acknowledgements *235*

FOREWORD

Vu Thi Ngoc Trang, the youngest of a relatively affluent family, was born in Ha Dong, North Vietnam, in 1946. The backdrop to her early childhood was Ho Chi Minh's war against France's efforts after World War II to resume its colony, known as French Indochina. Ho won his victory in 1954 and moved quickly to impose an oppressive regime that especially bore down on the professional and landowner classes, as well as the not inconsiderable Catholic communities. The Vu family had no choice other than to flee the north to start a new life in Saigon. It was there that Trang completed her primary and secondary education. An outstanding student, she won a Menzies Scholarship, under the Colombo Plan, to undertake tertiary studies in Australia. In 1964, when just eighteen, Trang arrived in Sydney from Saigon to take up her scholarship at the University of New South Wales (UNSW). By 1970 she had graduated with first-class honours in Psychology from UNSW and completed her master's at Macquarie University, also with honours.

Trang, with formidable dedication, pursued excellence in her psychology studies while working as a lecturer. Her most significant academic achievement was a PhD at La Trobe University in 1989 on psychology and care of the ageing. This ultimately led to her appointment as RMIT's first female professor. Soon after, there began a succession of appointments to public positions in the multicultural area, the first being an appointment for four years as Chair of the Victorian Multicultural Commission, a full-time position. Her daunting first task was to mediate a quarrel between two entrenched groups continuing to fight again ancient enmities from their Balkan origins. Trang began to make progress when she kept reminding the parties 'We are all Australians now'.

There followed a succession of important roles outside her academic career in various national bodies and inquiries, such as the Council for the Centenary of Federation, Constitutional Convention 1997-99 and inquiries into refugee children in detention. She also served as a member of the Board of the Special Broadcasting Service (SBS).

Her career both in academia and in public affairs spanned a period of vigorous growth and challenges in the transition from an Anglo-Celtic society to a multicultural Australia that encouraged participation by a very diverse range of people, cultures, faiths, races and talents. Professor Trang's success was the result of her passion for education, gained in part from her mother. It was achieved without any affirmative action, which demonstrates the wisdom of a society that provides opportunity to all without guaranteed outcomes. This book, beautifully written, with sensitivity and insight, recounts how parental values, an engaging personality and determination to succeed overcame problems of early disruption of war and the challenges of a quite diverse society.

The Trang story goes beyond a story of a migrant's success, for here was a migrant who not only achieved academic and public recognition in the wider community. She gave back to her new homeland - she lived out the subtitle of this book: *The More You Give*.

Sir James Gobbo AC

Melbourne, 29 July 2016

PREFACE

Australia, a nation built on colonisation and migration, is acclaimed as a success story for multiculturalism. Regrettably, this image is blemished by outstanding historical issues. Colonisation by the British from 1788 involved the displacement of Indigenous Australians from their traditional lands. Many of the consequences of European settlement are yet to be resolved.

The brighter side is that, in the mid-twentieth century aftermath of two world wars and severe economic depression, the fledgling nation commenced a large and sustained immigration program that continues today. The demise of the Eurocentric White Australia policy during the 1970s extended the scope of the program to include previously unwelcome newcomers. Since then, an influx of refugees from troubled and impoverished zones has contributed even further, amid a great deal of controversy over priorities and processes, to the diversity of Australia's population.

The nation has benefited hugely from the skills and determination to succeed displayed by its immigrants over many decades and by their Australian-born sons and daughters. Many have made extraordinary contributions to their adopted society. Leaders such as businessman Sir Arvi Parbo and pioneering surgeon Dr Victor Chang come readily to mind. But if one looks deeper into the pool of recognition there is a comparative dearth of immigrant women whose notable achievements have attracted nationwide attention. My aim in writing this biography is to ensure that one such eminent Australian, Emeritus Professor Trang Thomas AM, is not forgotten.

Trang arrived in Australia in the mid-1960s, a time of sweeping social change and a growing anti-authoritarian, anti-war movement. The imminent demise of the White Australia policy set the scene for the acceptance of increasing numbers of non-European immigrants. The second wave of feminism and the emerging reality of multiculturalism swept through the decades that followed, accompanied by the technological revolution that continues to transform communications, work practices and recreational preferences. Outdated social mores and rigidities based on traditional gender roles could no longer withstand scrutiny. The contraceptive pill gave women much more control over their fertility. Equal opportunity morphed from a dream to an imperative. Slowly but unstoppably, women were on the move to higher-level appointments.

For wide-eyed Trang, a refugee from Ho Chi Minh's communist regime at the age of eight, the Colombo Plan scholarship that enabled her to study in this new and very different society a decade later posed barriers ranging from Australian English to the prevalent casual racism that predated the era of political correctness. Determined to fit in to her new social environment, she set about making Australian friends and achieving highly as a student. Against the backdrop of her growing fear for her family's safety as war once more engulfed her native Vietnam, she succeeded beyond all expectations. Australia became her new and much-loved home. Along the way, her experiences and observations engaged her with the ideals of gender equality and multiculturalism that contributed so much to her future direction.

To shrink Trang's lifetime of adventure and achievement into this brief account has been a demanding task. Fortunately, the highlights of her career are matters of public record. For the remainder, she has been generous with her own account but at times too modest to take due credit for her numerous appointments to prominent professional and community service positions. I am therefore indebted to family members, friends and colleagues who have contributed their insights into Trang's roles as academic, multiculturalist, wife and mother. Along the way, her strong sense of duty and remarkable work ethic have enabled her to overcome many challenges in managing her multiple commitments. Her message to her young female students has been pragmatic and consistent. 'You can achieve many goals,' she assures them, 'but not always at the same time.'

On Trang's contribution to her new land, I can do no better than to quote Wendy McCarthy's words from *A Fair Go: Portraits of the Australian Dream*, (Focus Publishing, 1999), the stories of fifty notable immigrants published to mark the fiftieth anniversary of the Australian Citizenship Act 1948:

> For some the choice was accidental. For others, Australia was a land of opportunity and refuge. In all cases the Australians featured…have

contributed immensely to the multiculturalism and sophistication of Australian life, and as a nation, Australia is the richer for their decision to live here.

I, for one, am certainly the richer for knowing Trang.

Peter Nolan

Coolum Beach, 2019

- CHAPTER 1 -

We Are All Australians Now

Melbourne, March 1994

Trang was no stranger to media exposure. Her appointment as Chair of Victoria's Ethnic Affairs Commission had attracted much interest, not least because she was a woman in the male-dominated world of ethnic affairs. But today's headlines were extraordinary, hailing her successful mediation of the escalating conflict between Australia's Greek and Macedonian communities. Where others had failed, she had succeeded.

Now it was time to face the media pack that thronged outside her office at the Commission. Already she had been alerted to some early headlines, but she had not expected this immediate storm of publicity. She recalls the scene that greeted her:

> It was overwhelming, my first such experience. All of the TV and print media were there. I still have a photograph. We are standing there surrounded by cameras, everybody putting their microphones in front of me, asking me to tell the story. Then there was a poster by *The Age*, all about the new Ethnic Affairs chief managing to bring peace. It was the first week in my new job, a real baptism of fire.

It had indeed been a daunting experience, a reminder if one was needed that Australia's growing reputation as a showcase for multiculturalism was not easily earned. This optimistic picture of acceptance of ethnic and cultural diversity was blurred by history's unfinished business. In Australia and elsewhere, millions of immigrants settling in new and very different societies were faced with a common dilemma: 'How can I give unquestioning allegiance to my new home and accept its community values while maintaining a cultural identity instilled over centuries by the traditional practices, alliances and enmities of my country of origin?'

This dilemma was at the heart of the confrontation between the Greek and Macedonian communities that had demanded Trang's immediate attention. It was a classic example of unresolved political issues. Greece, whose northernmost province is called Macedonia, had long disputed the use of the same name by the neighbouring Socialist Republic of Macedonia, a member state of the Socialist Federal Republic of Yugoslavia. The dispute flared into open activism when, in 1991, the Yugoslav Federation collapsed and the former Socialist Republic of Macedonia was declared the newly independent Republic of Macedonia. The new republic's choice of name quickly became a major point of contention internationally. In Australia, the Greek community pressured state and federal governments to not recognise the new Balkan state under its chosen title. In an attempt to defuse the situation, Australia and other countries prevailed upon the Republic of Macedonia to include the words 'Former Yugoslav' to clarify its reference to 'Macedonia'. The new republic also agreed to amend its constitution to rule out territorial claims to any part of Greece. Following this compromise, Australia formally recognised the new state as the Former Yugoslav Republic of Macedonia (FYROM) on 15 February 1994.

As a means of defusing ethnic tensions, this diplomatic solution initially achieved little more than the creation of yet another unwieldy acronym. The Greek community was not appeased by the changes and the Macedonian community was outraged by the Greeks' negative response. The war of words between the two groups escalated rapidly, despite an appeal by Prime Minister Paul Keating for a mature response by Australians of Greek descent. His intervention was neither welcomed nor heeded. Instead, there was an unprecedented outbreak of violence between the communities that included attacks on each other's churches. Nationwide efforts to bring the warring parties together had failed. Inevitably there would be bloodshed, a situation that could not be tolerated.

In Victoria, home to large and vocal ethnic communities, Premier Jeff Kennett called upon his new ethnic affairs chief for a breakthrough. 'You sort them out' was his concise direction to Trang. As she set about the task, it was already clear to her that mediation of the dispute would be possible only if she could find a way to appeal to common interests and responsibilities instead of arguing about ingrained attitudes. It was time, she decided, for a new approach:

> The leaders were the key to resolution of the dispute, and the difficult but essential first step was to convince them to come together. Where others had failed, I managed to broker an agreement for three representatives from each side to meet on the neutral ground of the Commission. Even then my efforts were almost derailed. When the six community leaders arrived, they refused to enter the building. It was a very strained situation, but somehow I persuaded them to join me inside. I got them together in one room with drinks and food, and we talked. Since there was no point in trying to resolve their differences, my key tactic was an appeal to their sense of being Australians. I told them that this dispute must stop, that the conflict was over there in the Balkans and the communities here in Australia should not be fighting because we are all Australians now. Perhaps it was because I was a woman, a different voice with a broader viewpoint, but my approach began to bear fruit. Eventually, I got them to agree to a communique condemning the violence and calling for restraint. We achieved that late at night, I think the longest of my life.

Media curiosity was intensified by Trang's unprecedented achievement. 'Who is this Trang Thomas?' 'Where did she spring from?' The bare bones of her story were known, sparse details of a successful academic with an unusual background. Now there was respect and admiration. 'Who is this woman who has defied cultural norms by daring to challenge the right of influential old men to pursue older grievances?'

'We are all Australians now,' she had told the community leaders. Five simple words, a rare statement of clarity amid the evolving, politically correct jargon of inclusivity. Yet those five words described clearly her commitment to the nation that had offered her the opportunity to excel and the security of a permanent home. Her allegiance was born of experiences and influences that had driven her to give unstintingly of her best. Each is a story in itself, a building block in an inspiring life that began in the strife-torn north of Vietnam in the aftermath of World War II.

- CHAPTER 2 -

Origins

Hanoi, 2012

Although Trang had lived in Hanoi as a child, she found it hard to reconcile her images of that time with the sprawling city it had become over the decades since Ho Chi Minh's communist regime had imposed its brutal revolutionary principles. Arriving at her hotel in the Old Quarter, now a popular tourist destination, she was taken aback by the sheer density of population thronging the narrow, tree-lined, roughly paved streets where the members of tiny households spilled through their shopfronts to eat and gossip in the company of friends and neighbours. That custom was increasingly difficult to maintain. In these modern times there was a new, hugely intrusive element. The footpaths were clogged with parked motor scooters, a colourful barrier to pedestrian traffic. Locals and visitors alike struggled to find sitting or walking space, their chatter lost amid the incessant beeping of a thousand horns as scooters and cyclos weaved courageously among larger vehicles in a grinding, lurching tsunami that rolled inexorably through the streets. This was the street music of contemporary Hanoi, so different from the relative quiet of the orderly city she had known.

Trang loved to travel, make new friends and enjoy new experiences. On this occasion she was leading a group of Australian psychologists on a professional development tour of Vietnam. Her aim was to establish professional links with their Vietnamese counterparts and to discuss with them the significant barriers to the provision of mental health services in Vietnam posed by traditional beliefs and cultural practices. An understanding of these issues was particularly helpful to Australian practitioners whose work included the provision of services to Australia's large Vietnamese community. Scheduled activities also included presentations by tour group members on their own areas of specialty and particular case studies.

That night the group gathered in the hotel restaurant to dine and listen to Trang's briefing as she outlined the mix of professional and recreational activities she had planned for the following two weeks. Trang also introduced her eldest sister, Kim, who was making her first visit to Vietnam since she had fled from tragic family losses and persecution by the communist regime after the Vietnam War. She had invited Kim to join the tour so she was on hand to support her through potentially traumatic memories triggered by her recall of events so long ago. The group's travels would cover much of the country before culminating, far to the south, in Ho Chi Minh City. Trang had lived in that city, then called Saigon, for an eventful decade after her family fled from Hanoi in 1954. Most of the group knew little more about her origins.

Trang noted during her briefing that the psychologists and the sole psychiatrist in the group were all women, and that three of them were accompanied by their partners, including myself. Over dinner and drinks, my wife, Robyn, mentioned that I was a veteran of the Vietnam War and had since written a history of Australian Army Aviation's role in the conflict. Trang was quick to sense an opportunity to add an extra presentation to her program.

'Your knowledge and experiences should be shared with the group,' she told me. 'You will be my historian. On our bus trip to Ha Long Bay, I would like you to tell us about your experiences and what motivated you to write a history of the conflict.'

Given the circumstances, I could hardly refuse Trang's request. 'I suppose I could do something along those lines. Perhaps I could describe the conduct of counter-insurgency warfare and discuss some of the psychological effects on those who were involved. In return for my modest contribution, I'd like to ask a favour. The little I know about you suggests an extraordinary background. I'd be interested to hear more about your family's experiences here in the north while Ho Chi Minh's forces were fighting to defeat the French colonialists. And the partition of Vietnam after Ho's victory, of course.'

'That's fair enough,' Trang responded. 'I can't tell you much because I was so young. My elder sisters Kim and Chau know my early history much better than I do. You've already met Kim. I'm sure she'll tell you about it.'

Ha Dong, Vietnam, 1946

Trang was born Vu Thi Ngoc Trang into a world riven by the ideological and territorial conflict of World War II. It was 1946, her arrival coinciding with the beginning of the Cold War's escalating tension between communism and capitalism, the clash of ideologies perhaps an even greater force against peace than the thwarted imperial ambitions it replaced.

The postwar reshuffle of nations into a new world order also heralded the retreat by European powers from their colonial empires. In South-East Asia, a rising tide of anti-colonialism was quickly evident. It was time to dismantle the imperial structures of territorial gain and exploitation of less technologically developed societies. Trang's home country led the way, after Japan's defeat in World War II brought not only an end to its occupation of Vietnam but also a determined effort by France, sidelined during the war, to restore its hegemony over Indochina. Nationalist opposition to France's intentions by Ho Chi Minh's Viet Minh (Revolutionary League for the Liberation of Vietnam) triggered the First Indochina War and the eventual defeat of the French at Dien Bien Phu in 1954. This war was the backdrop for Trang's early childhood.

Born to a relatively affluent northern Vietnamese family, Trang was a product of two strong cultural influences. Her parents were both from the small village of Cu Da, not far from Hanoi. Her father, Vu Van Tung, was born in 1908, the first son of a wealthy landowner. Tung's upbringing was strictly traditional, his learning shaped by Chinese scholars so that, as an adult, he was highly respected as an authority on the cultural traditions of his people. In Vietnamese culture, high priority is given to the avoidance of bad luck. Men of Tung's status were consulted by the villagers and townspeople on the crucial process of selecting auspicious days for taking significant decisions on business and life matters.

As first son and heir designate of his family's estate, Tung was also deeply involved in his father's business affairs. His focus on his responsibilities to his tenants, family and village meant that, although he grew up under French colonial rule, he was not well informed about the world outside his traditional life. In this regard, he was very different from his wife. Trang's mother, Trinh Thi Binh, was the third daughter of a large and much more progressive middle-class family. Binh was French-educated. A high-achieving scholar, she might have gone far in an academic career. Instead, in accordance with tradition, her marriage to Tung was arranged soon after she graduated.

The marriage agreement was a protracted process. The two families had agreed that Binh and Tung should marry, although Binh's mother later expressed some strong reservations. In a change of mind, she said that her daughter was beautiful and educated and that Tung was not worthy of her. He was rich, but he had little knowledge of the Western world and new ways of thinking. Her daughter would have a brighter future married to someone better suited to her background. Tung's parents were not pleased with this argument. They insisted that Binh's family must keep their word or Tung's father would lose face with the people in his village. Losing face was a very serious matter.

Binh's father did not agree with his wife's change of mind. He was very unwilling to withdraw from the agreement because his family had already received so many gifts from Tung's family. He insisted that they must not swallow their words. It was difficult to resolve this situation. So Binh's mother came up with another plan. She asked Tung's family to pay a very high bride price, ten bars of gold, hoping they would withdraw from the negotiations. But Tung's father brought only five. She refused. 'No. Five is not enough. You must bring ten.' He met her demand and she finally agreed to the union. For the wedding day, the gold was made into jewellery for Binh, her arms and neck weighed down with dozens of gold bangles. Many years later, Trang was given one of those pure gold bangles to cherish in her memory. She has now passed it on to her daughter, Helen, hoping that it will remain in Australia forever, a family heirloom enjoyed by many generations of daughters.

Binh duly joined Tung in her father-in-law's large country household. She promptly met her obligations by producing their first child, not the much-anticipated first son but first daughter Dung. Amid many sighs of relief, the next child was first son Phuong. Childbearing aside, her life was very comfortable and comparatively idle. Servants provided for every need and there were cards and Mahjong to play with several unmarried aunts living in the household. That indulgence came to an end when Binh's mother visited one day and was horrified to find her modern, gifted daughter surrounded by servants and children being home-tutored, but doing little else. She immediately demanded that her daughter and son-in-law be set up in their own household in nearby Ha Dong, a small city eleven kilometres from Hanoi that was famous for producing the best silk in Vietnam. There the children could be properly educated in French schools. Her expectations of a large family were fulfilled. There would be six more offspring for a total of eight: Kim and Chau, second and third daughters; Quynh and Dzi, second and third sons; and, finally, Le and Trang, fourth and fifth daughters.

Grandmother was quick to instruct Binh in the textile business. With Tung's money, the young wife began trading in silks and cotton, and later moved on to clothing manufacture. She became a very astute businesswoman. It was to be the most settled time of the family's lives until, in the years before Le and Trang arrived, everyday life in Vietnam was interrupted by the outbreak of World War II and the subsequent occupation of the country by the Japanese. Kim, twelve years Trang's senior, remembers the challenges of this period:

> I was born in 1933 in Ha Dong, but at that time my family lived in my paternal grandfather's big country house in Cu Da. It was about seven kilometres from Ha Dong. So we older ones spent our early years there. When my older sister Dung and brother Phuong were ready for school, they needed to live in Ha Dong because there were no schools in our village. So we moved to the city, where Mother started a business and we were educated through elementary and middle school. Mostly my dad stayed in the countryside with my grandfather because his work as a landholder was there. Then World War II brought change. When the Japanese came to occupy our country we left Ha Dong. We moved further and further into the countryside until the hostilities were over and we were able to move to the capital, Hanoi, in 1947. By then the Japanese had been defeated and the French had come back to take over again. I remember that the whole family could not go to the city together. Chau and I were the first and then Kim Chi, our cousin, who lived with us. Mother and Dung and Trang were the

last ones to come. Before that Trang had stayed with her nanny in the countryside because she was only eight months old. Just a baby. And when all of us were reunited in Hanoi, Chau and I, with our two younger brothers, Quynh and Dzi, went to the French school. So we had a French education right through to university.

Despite the outward normality of their lives, Trang's parents were deeply troubled by the dark forces of change that stemmed from Ho Chi Minh's rise to power. Ho's beliefs and values were strongly grounded in the communist ideal. His campaign to oust the French was therefore integral to his plans to impose fundamental social and economic reform on his people. The professional and landowner classes were anathema to his rigid principles, and this attitude placed Trang's family under threat of persecution and forfeiture of their property. Her father's life would most likely be forfeit as well. But flight was not yet an imperative. Ho faced difficult odds against the French and victory was by no means certain. While there was doubt, the family would not leave. The north was their beloved home and, after the chaos of World War II, they had dared to hope they might be able to return to their former lives. So they settled in a large, rambling house on Silk Street, now the heart of Hanoi's tourist area. In conjunction with building up the family business, Mother prepared for the worst. She worked hard to increase their store of portable wealth as a hedge against the loss of property that was inevitable if Ho was victorious. Although she was not the head of the family, she was clearly its leader. Her values and strength would shape the lives of her eight children.

- CHAPTER 3 -

Childhood Memories

Hanoi, 1950-54

Trang was too young to understand in any detail the political and social implications of Ho Chi Minh's war against the French. Her first vague memories date from four years after her birth coincided with the beginning of Ho's struggle against colonialism in 1946. Her early childhood was typical for a child living in a family of respectable means, with one marked difference. Unlike their elder siblings, she and Le attended Vietnamese instead of French schools because Mother felt that the days of French influence were numbered. Le, two years Trang's senior, has stronger memories.

> The war didn't really touch us. I was five or six years old. I recall being carried on my nurse's back to go to kindergarten. I was kept back for a year so that Trang and I could go together. We were very close, always played together. We collected bits and pieces, because in those days there were no sophisticated toys. Mother ran a clothing factory at that time, so we could make dolls from rags we gathered there.

By then the household was quite large: a family of ten plus Trang's paternal grandfather; her eldest brother Phuong, now married with three children; cousin Kim Chi and her mother; and, not unusually, a number of other relatives. As well, there were nannies for each child, a cook and general servants. Importantly for Trang's future, Mother increasingly took the lead in family decisions. Her family would come to rely on her capacity for planning and organisation for their safety. And, in the longer term, it was her commitment to academic excellence that encouraged Trang to follow her siblings into higher education.

Nannies were of particular importance during early childhood. They were wet nurses as well, so the bonds that developed with their young charges could be particularly strong. However, their services could be transferred to another child and that could be upsetting. Le was almost two years old when Trang was born, and the decision was taken that Le's nanny would be responsible for Trang's care. Kim recalls that Le was not impressed when her nanny was reassigned to breastfeed Trang.

> She became a very difficult toddler, resisting attempts to wean her. It must have been a traumatic experience for her. To a Vietnamese child, her nanny was like a mother. Le's nanny was her sole carer for twenty-one months and then Trang arrived. But Le was so insistent on being fed that Nanny's breasts were smeared with chili to turn her off. And she would become so distressed that sometimes Nanny would take her off somewhere and feed her, just for a treat.

Trang's early memories are fleeting images of households and streets, faces and gatherings to observe ceremonies of ancestor worship, marriages and New Year celebrations. It was not until she attended primary school that she began to notice, as children do, that for her parents it was a time of growing uncertainty and fear of what the future might hold. As the war against the French progressed, Ho's power and the intimidation of the public by his followers grew steadily. Mother, who was very well read, hated the principles and ideals of communism. She remained convinced that, if Ho Chi Minh came to power, her family's situation would be untenable under such an ideologically severe regime. So, as Trang grew, she sometimes heard her parents discussing what they should do when, as by then seemed inevitable, Ho won his war and imposed his harsh model of social and economic reform.

Trang remembers that it was an exciting time for her, a time of engagement and discovery. The streets in their area were full of shops, many of which sold textiles. The business skills Mother had learned in Ha Dong once again served her well. On the ground floor of the house her clothing factory produced apparel for sale in her own shop. It was truly a family enterprise. After the clothes were made, family members all helped with the finishing touches. Especially buttons and buttonholes. Duties were allocated according to age and gender. The older females sewed the buttonholes, the younger females sewed on the buttons and the youngest children, including males, threaded cotton on needles and put them in pin cushions. And there was another side to the family gatherings that helped to set Trang on the road to higher learning. She recalls listening spellbound to the stories.

> These sessions in the factory when we helped put the finishing touches to garments were my source of wonderful information. My aunts often told us stories from novels that they read, regardless of whether they were suitable for children. So I listened to the story of Anna Karenina when I was about seven years old. As well, my brothers and sisters discussed what they learned at school. So I also acquired a lot of knowledge about science, history and geography. I think these memories illustrate the degree to which education was valued and shared in my family. As the youngest, one advantage that I enjoyed was that I soaked up knowledge like a sponge from my high-achieving siblings as well as the family elders.

Unfortunately, Trang did not enjoy school as fully as she might have. She was quite shy and had little self-confidence. She recalls being bullied by a girl who would pinch her because she was a plump child by Vietnamese standards.

> I have had this complex about my weight ever since. In contrast, Le was beautiful and highly intelligent, attracting nothing but praise. I have always loved her dearly, but as a child in her shadow I often felt that I was wanting.

At this time, adding to Trang's woes at school, she became aware that she was at the bottom of her family's hierarchy. In the Vietnamese tradition of primogeniture, the first son is highly privileged as the successor to his father. Date of birth and gender dictate the ranking order of the rest of the children, with sons favoured over daughters. Trang was the youngest of eight siblings and was female, so everyone was above her. Her best way forward was through education and a career, or to be outrageously beautiful and attract a rich man. 'Alas,' she smiles now, 'I was a quite chubby little girl. I would have to find another way.'

As Trang's awareness of her lowly status grew, she came to realise that her nanny was the rock who sheltered her from childhood fears and hurt. Her wet nurse from birth and her primary carer, Nanny was always there for her. That said, Nanny's key role in Trang's early life does not mean that her parents had no feelings for her. She doesn't recall that her father regretted her arrival or was ever unkind to her. Rather, she doubts that he gave her much thought at all given the weighty matters of business and future security on his mind. She was simply the last child, another mewling, unplanned arrival in an already large household. Nameless for several weeks until her sisters suggested that she be called Trang, she would grow up and go to school and get married and be a housewife and maybe run a business, or she wouldn't. It was not a matter that concerned him. Whatever happened to the family, there would always be a place for Trang, even as unattached female baggage. 'I grew up paying due respect to him,' she says, 'but didn't know him well enough to form properly the strong bond that underpins a daughter's love for her father.'

She was much closer to Mother. In the important roles of head of the household and businesswoman, Mother was much more engaged in Trang's upbringing despite the multiple demands of her work and home life. There were servants, of course, to cook and clean and care for the children, but it was Mother who oversaw the progress of all of her children from infancy to schooling and beyond. That she was an exceptional woman would become even more evident as the war drew towards its inevitable conclusion.

- CHAPTER 4 -

Flight from Hanoi

Vietnam's north, 1954

Trang was in her eighth year when Ho Chi Minh's forces finally defeated the French at Dien Bien Phu. Despite Ho's victory, Vietnam was far from being a unified nation elated by freedom from its colonial master. There was instead a deep rift between the political forces of the north and south that threatened the outbreak of civil war. A Geneva Conference was convened in May 1954 to seek a solution. After two months of negotiations, the nation was temporarily partitioned into North Vietnam and South Vietnam at the seventeenth parallel. The aim was to conduct a national election by 1956 to unite the country under one government. The agreement also provided for a 300-day period of grace during which free movement would permit citizens to choose between the two regimes. The border at the seventeenth parallel would then be sealed on 18 May 1955.

The grace period saw a huge exodus from the north. The French military, despite its defeat, assisted some 500,000 citizens to make the journey. The United States also provided passage for hundreds of thousands of people. Large numbers of the refugees were Catholics fearing religious persecution under Ho's communist regime. Many others, including Trang's family, were landowners and professionals who fled from the threat of persecution or death and the confiscation of their property.

With characteristic foresight, Mother had made her plans long before the exodus began. Her thorough preparations included the purchase of a house in Saigon and the consolidation of much of the family's wealth into gold and other portable valuables. The house in Saigon was rented out to provide extra income. When she judged it was time to begin the move, she sent first son Phuong to find a place for the family to stay until the house became vacant. When Phuong had made the arrangements, she bought plane tickets at huge black-market prices and sent most of her children to join him. Trang was given a box and told to pack whatever she could fit in to take with her to the airport. She was told to leave winter clothes behind because it was hot in Saigon all year round. Abandoning more valuable possessions, she lovingly filled her box with the rag dolls that she had made herself from wool scraps from the floor of their clothing factory.

Dung, as the eldest daughter, was placed in charge of the trip for her younger brothers and sisters. The parents stayed behind to see what more they could salvage from their business interests before joining their family. Aged just eight, and despite her eager anticipation of adventure in a new place, leaving Nanny was by far the most traumatic event in Trang's young life. Nanny had encouraged her when she felt overshadowed and had dried her tears when she was bullied at school. The bond between them was deep. Trang still recalls vividly Nanny hanging on to her legs and crying at the airport. Even then, as she shared the young woman's grief, Trang did not fully understand that her family would not be returning, or that she might never see Nanny again.

The flight south was a memorable but anxious interlude. 'What would Saigon be like? Where would she go to school? Was it really so hot?' Trang's mind was still racing when the aircraft settled onto the runway at Tan Son Nhat airport and the next phase of her life began.

Even while Mother's plans for the relocation of the family to Saigon were proceeding smoothly, the seeds of a new war were being sown. During the exodus, Ho moved quickly to consolidate his power in North Vietnam by intensifying his reign of terror. He confidently expected to win the planned national election as the bulk of Vietnam's population was under his control. However, the government of South Vietnam, led by Ngo Dinh Diem and backed by the United States, refused to play into Ho's hands by complying with the election plans. Hostilities escalated steadily during the late 1950s as Ho intensified his campaign for a unified Vietnam by creating the National Liberation Front (NLF) for South Vietnam. In response, the United States began a build-up of forces in support of the South Vietnam government. From this point, there was no turning back by either side. The long-running Second Indochina War (the Vietnam War) followed.

For the many refugees who had fled from the prospect of persecution under Ho's regime, the escalating conflict would bring renewed concerns during the 1960s and beyond. If Ho's forces were victorious, they would again face persecution. While this outcome seemed unlikely if the United States continued its support for South Vietnam, Ho had shown that he was a redoubtable foe. In the mid-1950s, as the Vu family began the transition to a new life in Saigon, these concerns were still some years in the future. In the meantime, there were many more pressing issues to confront as refugees in a new and sometimes unfamiliar cultural setting.

The Vu sisters, Hanoi, 1950.
Trang (centre), aged four, with sisters Le, Dung, Chau and Kim.

Young refugees, Trang and Le with a rare doll in Saigon, 1955.

Trang's beloved Nanny, Hanoi, early 1950s.

- CHAPTER 5 -

Saigon

Saigon, 1954-64

Trang's eldest brother, Phuong, had rented the upper floor of a house, a very large empty room, as temporary accommodation until the little band of refugees could occupy their own house. During the days, they sat on mats to play, write and eat their meals. When night fell, they would set up camp beds and sleep head to toe. Le and Trang shared one such bed. Very soon both were enrolled in the local girls' school, bringing a measure of normality but also unforeseen challenges stemming from their status as refugees.

It would take another six months to complete the move to Saigon. First son Phuong and first daughter Dung returned to Hanoi to help their parents. Kim, aged twenty-one, was left in charge as the head of the Saigon household. She managed the money, carried the keys and was responsible for the younger children's nurture and schooling. Phuong's wife, Nhan, was responsible for feeding the family. Trang explains Nhan's role.

> She would give all of the orders to the servants - what we were going to eat today and what was needed for the daily shopping. We were allowed to use the landlord's kitchen on the ground floor. Our food had to be bought fresh every day at the market, of course, because in those days we had no refrigeration.

To a Westerner, the Saigon household described by Trang might seem quite unusual in terms of its hierarchy and division of responsibilities. Nhan, the eldest female and the mother of three children, would logically be left in charge. However, that would have been very much contrary to Vietnamese cultural tradition. When a son marries, it is usual that the new wife will come to live with his family. It is a period of transition, when she learns how to manage a household by starting on the bottom rung of the ladder. An important part of her apprenticeship is to learn to run the kitchen. This does nothing to elevate her in the household hierarchy. Typically there is an extended family: aunts, uncles, unmarried daughters. And of them all the new bride has the lowest status. Although Nhan had been Phuong's 'new wife' for years, her position in the hierarchy was thus unchanged.

Trang tells of an aunt who had found herself in this situation. At the dinner table, where seating was in strict order of rank, the new bride's place was the furthest from the head. Her job at mealtimes was to manage the rice pot, and to fill each person's bowl as it was handed to her. By the time she had served the last person but herself, the first would often have an empty bowl and so must be served again. Sometimes she would get little to eat before the rice bowl was empty, and on such occasions she would leave the table hungry. Whenever the opportunity arose, she would go home to her mother's house and have a big meal.

Such arrangements often lasted for several years until the bride had her own children and the new family set up their own household. Nhan was no doubt relieved when Phuong later found them a new home in Saigon. She was by then the mother of four. Interestingly, the birth of her fourth son raised another cultural issue unfamiliar to an outsider. In contrast to Western practice, the Vietnamese tradition is that a child should not carry the name of an ancestor back to five generations. But it was a chaotic time and there was nobody to consult about which names to avoid. The child was therefore given a most unusual name to avoid any offence to his forebears.

Meanwhile, the exodus from North Vietnam was gaining pace as time drew short. Trang's parents, and those of their Hanoi household who had not already moved to Saigon, left Hanoi for its port city, Haiphong. Once there, Phuong opened a pharmacy, where Mother traded gold between those who were staying and those who were leaving. She made a lot of money, so they stayed in Haiphong until the last days of the period of free movement before boarding an American ship to join their family in Saigon. On arrival, their next priority was to move from their temporary accommodation to Mother's now-available small house. Again they slept on mats on the floor, sometimes up to ten in a corner, as other relatives who had not yet found accommodation joined them. Despite the numbers, Mother ensured that all were fed by spending whatever was necessary on food. Trang recalls that the Americans also distributed food to refugees, including huge tins of yellow cheddar cheese that few people could eat. Although generous, the Americans did not understand that many stomachs around the world did not share their gastronomic fortitude.

Once again, Mother's business acumen provided the answer to the problem of overcrowding. She used the money she had made during those last six months in Haiphong to buy a larger home. The children still shared rooms, but there was enough space to accommodate extended family members who stayed while they were building their own new lives in Saigon. However, the resolution of the accommodation problem could not address other obstacles to resettlement. The psychological trauma of being uprooted from their relatively comfortable middle-class lives in the north posed particular problems. Trang recalls that her early days at the local schools were hurtful and frustrating:

> I could not understand the southern accent at first and I was smacked on my palms a few times for not following the teacher's instructions. It was the same language, of course, but there was the accent and there were idiomatic expressions as well. Just like in every country, as I later learned the hard way here in Australia. At school in Saigon we were jeered at as refugee kids. Even in the broader community the French policy of divide and conquer had left a legacy of hostility between the different ethnic groups of the north and south. My sister Chau told me that some of the Saigon students maybe felt a little resentful because it was always said that the girl from the north is more beautiful, more elegant because her skin is whiter. In the south, many people are descendants of the dark-skinned Cham people. I was not so beautiful, but Le was. So a lot of the girls picked on her.

Le and Trang were saved from the harassment they experienced when the continuing influx meant there were too many refugee children to be accommodated in regular classes at local schools. New schooling arrangements were set up for them, in which their teachers were also refugees and thus more sensitive to their needs. But beyond that there were no facilities, no new buildings. Instead, their schooling took place during the siesta breaks for the regular students, whose school hours were 7-11 am and 2-6 pm. The refugee school hours were thus between 11 am and 2 pm. For years Trang and Le had early lunch before going to school but they were much happier. Trang started to learn both French and English in Grade 5 and the Americans contributed generous quantities of books and stationery. These supplies included propaganda materials about the wonderful land of the United States, so she acquired a good deal of knowledge about that country's culture and geography. The French also wanted to maintain their cultural influence by supplying books. So Trang's first English textbooks were actually published in France. The Americans soon put an end to the French efforts by insisting that all textbooks must come from the United States. For the students, this cultural jostling was just another confusing aspect of growing up in a land of competing interests.

As the younger children's school years progressed, work and study dominated the lives of their older siblings. Phuong's qualifications enabled him to start a successful pharmacy business that in turn enabled him to build his own house. Dung had married in Hanoi before the exodus. She and her husband, Chuong, had also come to Saigon and now worked in the pharmacy with Phuong and Nhan. Quynh and Dzi, the other two sons, studied medicine and graduated as doctors. Elder sisters Kim and Chau graduated as pharmacists. Mother had long insisted that all of her children become healthcare professionals. 'No matter what happens or where you go,' she would say, 'people will always need care.' And because they all studied under French lecturers, their degrees were recognised in France.

Given this family background, it is not surprising that both Le and Trang were highly motivated students who went on to win scholarships under the Colombo Plan established after World War II to foster closer relations between British Commonwealth nations and other countries in the Asia–Pacific region. Winning a scholarship to study in countries like Australia and Canada was a highly competitive process. Surprisingly, it was Le who got off to a poor start.

> I worked very hard, but I was always very nervous when we went for a test. I would get into a real sweat over exams. I just couldn't do all

the work. I even failed twice, while Trang just sailed through. We were not in the same class. She was one year behind me. But I failed my year twice and had to go to a different school for the next four years. And after those four years I worked really hard and got into a better school. There were two high schools for girls in Saigon. Mine was really big. My best years were the last three years of high school, when I came top of my class. But I had to work so hard.

There was life outside school, of course. Trang and Le were typical teenagers and with their friends attended every Hollywood movie they could. They bought and treasured magazines with pictures of movie stars. At other times they visited libraries, just to hang out with their friends and take advantage of the free English classes offered by the Americans. But there were no boyfriends. That would have been seriously out of order.

It was a time of growing anxiety for millions of South Vietnamese, including the Vu family. By the early 1960s, the schism between North and South Vietnam had led inexorably to a buildup of forces on both sides with the strong backing of the greater powers involved in ideological conflict. What might have remained a civil war was inevitably doomed to be a proxy for the Cold War. The chain of events that led to this situation reflected the fear and mistrust of the great powers of the new world order. The domino theory of incremental communist expansion through the subjugation of smaller nations became the rationale for the ever-increasing involvement of the United States in Indochina.

On the international scene, the war of words was translating into action. In January 1961, Soviet President Nikita Khrushchev pledged support for wars of national liberation worldwide. Ho Chi Minh was greatly encouraged in his aim of unifying Vietnam as a communist state. The United States responded accordingly. In February 1962, the United States Military Assistance Command for Vietnam was established to support the gradual escalation of American military involvement. By the end of 1964, American military advisers numbered 23,000. Meanwhile, Australia's involvement had begun in July 1962 with the commitment of the Australian Army Training Team Vietnam (AATTV) to work with South Vietnamese forces against the estimated 170,000 Viet Cong and North Vietnamese Army soldiers already waging coordinated attacks against ARVN troops in the Saigon area. The stage was set for the further escalation of hostilities that became the Vietnam War.

During this period, life in Saigon remained relatively secure. It was only after Le had won her scholarship and departed for Australia in 1963 that Trang was disturbed by one of the war's saddest manifestations. The self-immolation of Buddhist monks protesting against actions by South Vietnam's Ngo Dinh Diem regime in 1963 attracted media attention worldwide. Trang, foreshadowing her lifelong commitment to fighting injustice, joined a street protest in support of the monks' cause. Her picture appeared in the newspaper the following day, no doubt causing her family considerable angst. It was a difficult period for her. She was missing Le badly. Le had been her constant companion since early childhood and it was inconceivable that she was now so far away. Fortunately, her brother Dzi stepped up to help fill the gap. Knowing that Trang too was studying hard to compete for a scholarship, he spent a lot of his time coaching her about Western culture and improving her general knowledge of science and history.

All too soon, it seemed, she graduated from secondary school with outstanding results and won her scholarship. What had been a possibility became reality as she too prepared to leave the growing threat to take up her studies in Australia. Sadly, while her departure was a physical escape, it raised rather than reduced her concerns. The war and its eventual devastating effects on her family would be uppermost in her thoughts for much of the next twenty years. But, for the present, she was distracted by excited anticipation of the adventures to come during tertiary studies in a new land.

CHAPTER 5 - Saigon

Father Tung, mother Binh, Trang and Le, visit Kim's boarding school at Da Lat, South Vietnam, 1956.

Left: Le and Trang prior to Le's departure for Sydney in 1962 to take up her Colombo Plan scholarship.

Above: Prizewinner Trang and mother at Trang's high school graduation, Saigon, 1963.

Trang with her parents, prior to her departure for Sydney in October 1964 to take up her Colombo Plan scholarship.

The Vu family gathers for Trang's farewell party, October 1964.

- CHAPTER 6 -

Place where the Sun Rises

Istanbul, 2012

Trang was happy to be travelling again, this time leading a professional development tour through Turkey. When the tour group gathered in Istanbul, she was pleased to see a number of familiar faces from the tour of Vietnam earlier in the year. I was among them, once again happy to accompany Robyn and hoping to learn more about Trang and her family.

Trang greeted us warmly. 'Welcome to Istanbul. I really enjoyed your company on our last tour. And it is good to have my historian again. It so happens that we are going to visit Gallipoli. It is a five-hour bus trip and, if you would be so kind, perhaps you could talk to us about the campaign there in 1915. The Anzac story is such an important part of Australian history and tradition now, as if it marks the time when we truly became a nation.'

I nodded slowly. 'I can do that. I've actually been reading up on Turkish history and World War I. It was a truly horrible conflict. Gallipoli was a tragic debacle, but the story of the Western Front almost defies belief. So many lives sacrificed, such indifference to suffering and loss by the generals and their political masters.'

'Yes,' she agreed. 'It was a terrible time for the survivors as well. So many injuries, so much undiagnosed psychological damage. But let's talk of happier times. Have you been to Turkey before?'

'No. I'm really looking forward to our time in Istanbul and visits to Cappadocia and the old cities of Ephesus and Hierapolis. It's a fascinating country, often described as one of the great crossroads of ancient civilisations. The whole place reeks of history. I much prefer its Greek name, Anatolia. It means "place where the sun rises". And, speaking of history, maybe you can tell me a little more of your own along the way. Perhaps, when you were leaving the darkness of escalating conflict in Vietnam, you thought of Australia as the place where the sun rises?'

'I don't recall thinking of it in that way,' she smiled, 'but I certainly saw it as a very different place, a land where I could learn so much. I was so excited.'

Sydney Airport, October 1964

So much that was new clamoured for Trang's attention in a haze of first impressions as her wide eyes took in the long concourse of Sydney Airport and the welcoming throng that surrounded her group. She was tired, of course, not so much from jetlag as an overdose of nervous speculation about this new land. Her student group had taken off from Tan Son Nhat International Airport just a day earlier, a relatively short flight by Pan American to Singapore for a brief stopover and then the excitement of boarding an Alitalia aircraft for the overnight flight to Sydney. Before that there'd been her farewell, and packing her baggage of treasured memories to cling to during the years of separation ahead. Her family, her girlfriends, all of them crying, and she too was crying and laughing and crying again. Still weeping on the aircraft, as if by the act of boarding she had somehow destroyed her links to all that had gone before.

She was one of a group of twenty Colombo Plan students. At Singapore, they'd gone into the city for the brief reassurance of final shopping in Asian surroundings before departing for a very different country. Most of the passengers already on the aircraft were Italian migrants, a surprise for the students because they knew little about Australia's large postwar immigration program.

For Trang, the one familiar face in the welcoming party at Sydney Airport was Le, now in her second year in Australia. She and Trang had looked forward immensely to their reunion. Le remembers the occasion well:

> We even planned to dress up in the same clothes, because at home we wore the same dresses, the same materials. Some of the Sydney papers came to the airport. They took our picture and next day it appeared in

the papers saying "Together Again!" It was so nice, and I'm sorry now that I didn't keep a copy.

Trang too was bemused by the photograph and feature story on the front page of the *Sydney Morning Herald*. She had been greatly comforted by Le's presence because she had not expected to be the centre of attention. It had all felt a little unreal.

After the photographs had been taken and the journalists moved on, Le had introduced Trang to her new hosts. The two ladies were very kind. They told Trang that they belonged to the Salvation Army. In her experience, armies had been synonymous with violent struggle, but not against sin. Yet it was not a big step for her to understand that this particular Christian army was engaged in good works. One of the ladies, Miss Gale, owned the house in Marrickville where Trang would join Le as another of several student boarders. It would be a novel experience to live in an Australian household, but there was little time to think of that now.

Leaving the airport, the drive to her host's home was a brief introduction to suburban Sydney, a sprawling city of two million. Accustomed to the warm climate, flat terrain and busy, communal street life of Saigon, Trang was unprepared for Sydney's undulating, comparatively quiet suburban streets and the chilly wind that knifed into her even on this spring day of October 1964. And now the first sight of her new home on a spacious block of land, quite unlike the city dwellings of her native Vietnam. She wished that her English was better, that she could understand and respond adequately to the words of welcome and support offered in the nasal twang of the local dialect. She had prepared herself for such obstacles, but it was impossible not to look back with longing to the comforting familiarity of native language and custom.

Despite her tiredness and the welcoming warmth of her bed, sleep was slow to come on that first long night, the tears that dampened her pillow persisting even as she wiped them impatiently from her cheeks. She was lonely, the distractions provided during the long journey by her fellow students no longer blocking the thoughts of home. There had been laughter and shared apprehension, then the heightened anticipation of discovery as journey's end neared. But now Trang was alone with her thoughts. She was just eighteen, and so much had happened since the war that liberated her country from the French had made her a refugee from Ho Chi Minh's regime in North Vietnam. To be here in Sydney, just a decade later, was overwhelming. She was at once fearful and excited, hoping beyond hope she could meet the expectations that now, in the quiet darkness of her room, seemed so unwontedly optimistic.

She blocked out the negative thoughts, trying to focus on the promise of new opportunities that would flow from her studies and the rewards of taking her place in an adult world. But her mind stubbornly took her back, past the decade of Saigon to the lingering memories of Hanoi. She wondered why, then realised that she was missing Nanny, the rock who had always brought comfort and reassurance when she was afraid. She finally drifted into an uneasy sleep, the images of her childhood still flickering at the edge of her consciousness.

Trang prepares to commence her first year studies at the University of New South Wales.

- CHAPTER 7 -

Induction

Sydney, October 1964 - February 1965

Trang woke early to her second day in Sydney, her mind still churning with the restless images of the dawn dreaming. Reality struck almost immediately, the intrusive thoughts of long ago crowded out by nervous anticipation of the time to come. She was here in Australia, a teenage girl from a divided country once more sinking rapidly into deadly conflict. She must try to put concerns about home and family aside for the moment to concentrate on overcoming any obstacles to making the most of her opportunity. Today would be the first full day of an experience that must surely bring challenges that even Mother, that strong and confident woman, would approach with trepidation. Trang had won a coveted Colombo Plan scholarship, yes, but was she smart enough to meet the educational standards in this new country?

Her sister Le, now in her second year at the University of Sydney, was doing well. But that thought was small comfort. Le had always been the clever one, and the prettiest. She had worked very hard for her student position in Sydney, even coming first in nationwide examinations. Trang recalled again how often she herself had been introduced as a high achiever, only to hear the speaker go on to say: 'But you should meet her sister, Le! She has it all!'

A gentle knock on her door dispelled Trang's brief lapse into pessimism. She threw aside the bedclothes, remembering to greet Miss Gale in English as she entered. Her landlady's bright, inquisitive eyes took in every detail of Trang's appearance as she held out a glass of orange juice. 'Big day today,' she smiled. Trang drank her juice, an unexpected kindness, thinking that today might indeed be quite large and now, in a burst of optimism, looking forward keenly to the new experiences it would bring.

An hour later she was taken by officials from the Commonwealth Office of Education, along with the other two girls who had been allocated to the same lodgings, to join the rest of their group for a day of orientation in Sydney. As Colombo Plan students, they were well looked after. The plan had been established in 1945, initially as a means for developed British Commonwealth nations to assist their less developed counterparts. A number of non-Commonwealth nations later joined and expanded its scope. Six countries (Britain, Australia, New Zealand, Canada, Japan and the United States) now supplied aid to twenty less developed countries. For Australia, the plan was an important foreign affairs initiative, the nation's first serious postwar attempt to engage with its neighbouring Asian countries despite the discriminatory barrier of its White Australia policy.

Much of this Trang learned later, of course. When she arrived, she didn't yet understand the complexities of Australia's postwar immigration program or why New Australians, as they were called, were predominantly from European countries. She was simply thankful for the chance to study in a safe place, hoping that the situation in her own country would be resolved by the time her studies were completed and it was time to return to Saigon.

She quickly became engrossed in her induction program. During those first few months before the beginning of the 1965 academic year, the new students were given English lessons, a crash course at the Sydney Technical College in Sussex Street. They went every day so it was their major activity. In addition to the language classes, there was a limited choice of subjects related to what they were going to study at university. Trang took psychology and philosophy. The teachers were very effective because they specialised in teaching foreign students. They were conscious of language difficulties and confusion made worse by the unthinking use of rapid, slurred speech in the Australian idiom. Trang enjoyed too those aspects of the program that took them out of the classroom into the community. Her group was taken on a range of outings, which included a visit to the Holden car factory and a trip to the Blue Mountains. Every weekend they were taken out to see another tile in the Australian mosaic.

The end of 1964 brought the unfamiliar celebrations of Christmas and New Year. Trang and Le enjoyed taking part, but for them it was the festival of Tet, the Chinese New Year celebration later in January, that marked the real beginning of what was Trang's first full year in Australia. Then, in February, the new students were divided into smaller groups according to their chosen study programs. Some went to study at the University of Western Australia. Another group went to Brisbane. Trang and three or four others had been accepted into the University of New South Wales (UNSW). Trang recalls that she would have liked to join Le at Sydney University.

> At that time it was very hard for foreign students to gain admission to the University of Sydney. Le had been accepted on the strength of her academic record, but the majority of us went to UNSW. This is not to say that UNSW was second rate. It was just that the University of Sydney was older and more prestigious.

As she farewelled her friends of the past four months and prepared to begin her studies, Trang mentally squared her shoulders. Everything had gone well so far. Now it was her turn, her time to excel. She felt she had much to prove and anything less than impressive results would be unacceptable. Whatever the obstacles, she would find a way around them. But she was glad for Le's continuing presence, an ever-comforting link to the past they had shared so closely. 'What if we had not won scholarships?' she wondered. 'What would we be doing now if we had stayed in Saigon? Studying pharmacy, probably, following in the footsteps of our elder sisters. Or preparing for marriage to suitable candidates.' Looking back, it seemed that family traditions were little changed by the decade since they had fled from Hanoi. Yet almost everything else had. She had escaped the unrest and uncertainties of her homeland, at least temporarily, but it seemed she had joined a quite different society, one that was busily shedding the bonds of tradition to embrace new freedoms and diversions.

Trang has always been very observant, and her observations unfailingly stimulate her curiosity. Not surprisingly, she was mindful of her early experiences as a refugee in Saigon as she began to build a mental picture of her new environment. Now she faced a second and more intense culture shock. She had arrived at a time of social revolution throughout the West, a period of radical change that was already reshaping Australia's sociocultural structure.

As a modest young lady accustomed to the strict behavioural boundaries of her upbringing, Trang was fascinated by the new attitudes and social norms. The 1960s introduced a new, permissive age of unprecedented sexual freedom accompanied by a surge in the use of recreational drugs. And there was much more than sexual experimentation, the contraceptive pill, pot and LSD. Not only was the book of social mores being rewritten, but the sheer breadth of new trends in entertainment, fashion and lifestyle choices was also remarkable. Bikinis flowered on Australia's white beaches while its youth embraced the surfing culture. More young women began to question both the desirability and the inevitability of marriage, children and life as a housewife. Across the land, parents were distraught and confused as they tried in vain to raise their children in conformity to attitudes and practices entrenched by decades of war, economic hardship and the dictates of religious dogma. It was a losing battle.

Viewed through the prism of Trang's cultural background, her early impressions of the Australian society would inevitably influence the directions and passions she would follow in adult life. She was already intrigued by the roles, attitudes and limited expectations of women she had thus far met. She would learn much more about such matters during her student years, but first she must focus on her studies. Improving her English, she decided, was of much greater concern than understanding the noisy rhythms of social, economic and political change.

- CHAPTER 8 -

First-Year Studies

University of New South Wales, 1965

For Trang, it was a moment to lock into her memory. She was at last a university student, breathing the expectant air of academe, eager to take the next steps on her road to scholarship and success. But first there were practicalities to address, in particular enrolment in the courses she had chosen and finding her way around the broad campus.

Alert and self-conscious, she found a measure of comfort in numbers as she joined the stream of students embarking on their own tours of familiarisation. No one seemed to take much notice of her Asian appearance. Many chatted amiably in pairs and small groups, their interaction very casual and relaxed in this much more egalitarian society. Trang would find as the days passed that not only her fellow students but also her lecturers and tutors spoke to her quite informally.

As she had expected, the most significant barrier to high achievement in her studies was the language. She spoke and read well, but her listening and writing skills lagged behind her other competencies. Her worst fears were realised when she attended her first classes. For the most part, lectures were delivered in quite rapid speech in the broad Australian accent that often defied understanding. Clearly she could not raise her hand or jump to her feet every few minutes to request a slower and more carefully enunciated presentation. What to do? All she could think of was to get used to the Australian version of English by exposing herself to more of the same. As she explains:

> Asian girls tend to hang out together. You'll see groups of them, students of the same origin. But I made the decision very early that I would not

seek out someone who spoke my language. Instead, I would mix with the Australian students and make friends among them. If I could learn to understand Australian English as well as showing them that Asian girls were just girls it would be a big step forward. So at lunchtimes I would mix with them, meeting some very kind friends along the way. I remember a Salvation Army officer who'd been sent there to study social work. He was in the same class with me in psychology. He was a mature-age student, very determined to do well. At the end of every lecture he would type up his notes and give me a copy. Fortunately my reading skills were much more advanced than my listening skills. He was not the only one who helped me. In those days I really felt that I owed much of my progress to my Australian friends. The rest I could owe to my serious approach to study. I did not yet have any kind of social life, so every night I would sit down with Le and do my homework. We seldom went out. Studying was our life.

Trang took courses in psychology, French, sociology, and the history and philosophy of science. The latter subject focused on the development of astronomy from early studies of the planets and neighbouring stars. She had been interested in the wonders and mysteries of the universe from childhood, when her brother Dzi had taught her a lot about these matters. She recalls:

We learned about Copernicus, Galileo, Kepler, those great minds that contributed so much to the advance of astronomy. And my results were very good because all of the exams and tests were multiple-choice. I had what is called a graphic memory. I would study the textbooks and, if I could recall where answers were in a textbook, whether it was top or bottom or left on the page, I could produce the answer from memory. That was partly because, in Vietnam, we were given education which involved a lot of rote learning, remembering chunks of information and where they were in the textbook. Those skills enabled me to do well except when it came to essays. That was a disaster. I remember that my tutor used to say that my English was hilarious. It was just the way I expressed it, not in any way how English people would express the same material. On the other hand, I continued to get very high marks in any subjects that had multiple-choice tests. It was fortunate that by the end of first year I decided to specialise in psychology. The department at UNSW at that time placed a great deal of emphasis on applied psychology. This involved many multiple-choice tests but comparatively few assignments in the form of essays. So it suited me and I did very well. From then, most of my subjects at university were to do with psychology and by my third year I was studying it full time.

Trang was also very good at statistics, a key skill for research projects and for her a pleasing combination of numbers and logic. One of her lecturers, after marking a test, walked in and asked, 'Who is this student whose mark is one standard deviation above the next student?' And then another lecturer said, 'Who is this Chinese girl who knows everything?' Trang was saved from embarrassment by a friend who responded firmly on her behalf. 'First of all she is not Chinese, and secondly she doesn't know everything.' Trang wasn't sure about the second statement but was grateful for her friend's support. It made her feel that she belonged.

Fortune smiled on Trang in another way. She found an enthusiastic and caring mentor in Dr Una Gault, a single academic who took lost little girls under her wing. Dr Gault offered support and guidance to the young Vietnamese student, who still gives her credit for much of her subsequent success in her studies. 'She was very honoured among women, well known for her caring and her dedication to women's causes.'

Trang supposed that her progress as a high-achieving student helped her to be accepted by her fellow students. But, although she was pleasantly surprised by the lack of overt hostility to her as an Asian, it was clear to her from very soon after her arrival that she was regarded by her peers as someone unusual and unexpectedly bright, rather than being accepted without question as an equal. She had come prepared to encounter prejudice, in part because of her memories of being treated with hostility as an outsider when she was a schoolgirl refugee in Saigon. After all, she reasoned, if bias and prejudice were so evident in her own country, why should she expect uncritical acceptance and tolerance here in a new and very different society? This was the West and, in the long history of Western dealings with the Orient, through exploration and colonisation and war, there seemed to be no hint that the people of the East were regarded as civilised equals. Not by the French, British or Australians, certainly. The Chinese had invented gunpowder and created fine ceramics, yes, but they were definitely not equals. They were commonly identified with idols, cunning business practices, joss sticks and opium dens. Those Chinese who had come to Australia much earlier, during the nineteenth-century gold rushes, were best known as operators of laundries and market gardens. They ate rice instead of proper food like mutton and potatoes. Not the sort of people you would welcome unreservedly into your circle, let alone marry.

Overhearing such comments, no matter how casually and good-naturedly expressed, led Trang to question how much of the tolerance and acceptance she was presently being shown was a veneer, a thin mask of pretend courtesy that was donned only in her presence. It wasn't a good thought. And then it struck her that perhaps people of all nations welcomed others only for the advantages that might be gained from interaction rather than with genuine feelings of warmth and friendship. She quickly rejected that thought, because it meant she could only find genuine acceptance within her own ethnic group and, if that was true, why was she here? What was the point of the Colombo Plan? Or of Australia's expanding immigration program? It was very confusing, she thought. It was all too easy to question what she might instead take for granted, but too hard to take for granted that others might come to love her just for being herself.

She eventually reached the conclusion that, in deciding her response to any hostility or bias she experienced, it was necessary to draw a line in the sand. If she encountered attitudes and actions that threatened the completion of her studies, she would fight hard to hold her ground. But if words and actions were merely hurtful, regardless of intent, then she would ignore them or show by example that they were wrong. That would be her plan until she learned more through experience. The frustrating part was that, even if she found someone who could help her to clarify her situation, she did not yet have the fluency to discuss such issues in English. In a way this was surprising, because her sister Le had not experienced the same linguistic difficulties. Obviously, Le's choice of an arts degree would have exposed her more quickly to the creative aspects of written language. As well, she recalls attending many English tutorials during her orientation period after her study preferences became known. For whatever reason, it seems that Le either had a higher aptitude for languages or came to Australia more confident in her skills.

For her part, Le recalls that, while her own listening and writing skills were advanced, she was very nervous about speaking to a group. In contrast, Trang was a bubbly and confident speaker. As Le explains:

> I remember that the Salvation Army ladies used to ask us sometimes to give talks about Vietnam. I was always so nervous. But Trang wasn't. So I would write something and let her make the speech. I didn't really see her as having any academic problems. She was so determined. I used to tell her that she was an overachiever. Maybe it was because she was the youngest in the family. But I've always seen her as the youngest, smartest and most successful of all the siblings. And such a very generous person, too.

Through all of this period of adjustment to her new circumstances, Trang's thoughts were never far from home because of the war. It was 1965 and the build-up of forces was continuing. Australia was sending an infantry battalion and support units to join the American forces at Bien Hoa. That was quite close to Saigon, so the threat to the southern capital, and with it her family, must be increasing. She felt helpless, but continued to apply herself to her studies because the future was so full of uncertainty. She must be prepared for any eventuality.

The end of first-year studies came with its usual rush of last-minute preparation for examinations, with Trang acquitting herself very well. Her competence in her non-psychology electives helped her to a high standard across the board. In French, for example, from previous exposure she wasn't shy about talking in French to the tutors. In the first year she left most of the class behind because of her relative fluency. Similarly, she did very well in her studies of the history and philosophy of science, and decided to take this subject again in second year. So, in all, she did not find her university studies difficult except for the relatively slow development of her English language skills. That remained her major concern, the barrier she must overcome. The summer break from university studies meant she would see little of her first-year friends, but it did open up other avenues for development of her listening skills while learning more about her new society. Rather than waste her time feeling lonely and homesick, she worked as an assistant nurse at a small maternity hospital run by the Salvation Army. She recalls that the experience intensified her curiosity about the position of women in society and attitudes to the young girls 'ruined' by premarital sex:

> I found that about half of the patients were unmarried mothers. The married patients were called the ladies, the unmarried ones the girls. The latter would come from all over New South Wales to have their babies and then give them up for adoption. The process was quite an eye-opener. I would just get to know the girls, seeing them arrive pregnant to have their babies, and then they would be off again, dressed in nice clothes, picked up by their boyfriends. And the babies would be left behind. It was hard for me to understand that this was an accepted part of life in Australia.
>
> My job was to look after the babies, to change their nappies and feed them. Because the girls were leaving their babies behind, breastfeeding was not allowed. Sometimes, on rare occasions, the mother decided she wanted to keep the baby. Then she would get special treatment, and be allowed to breastfeed. Then there were others who just didn't want to even see the baby in their haste to leave. I was surprised so many didn't seem to be upset or overly concerned by their experience. They would just get dressed in their good clothes, put on their makeup and leave to get on with their lives. There was the hint of an assembly line about the whole process. As quickly as the girls departed, the adoptive parents would arrive with beautiful clothes, waiting while we dressed the babies in their new finery and leaving happily with their treasures.

Reflecting on her summer of 1965, Trang is struck by the extent of change over the decades since. Much of the community disapproval of unmarried mothers and their children has dissipated in the context of a less judgemental, more liberal society, while support pensions give young mothers the means to keep their babies. Paradoxically, it is adoption, once the widely accepted means of leaving disgrace and difficulty behind, that has now replaced the perceived stain of illegitimacy as a situation contrary to the interests of mother and child. Indeed, the pendulum has swung so far that to gain approval for adoption is not only a very difficult process but also one that attracts widespread condemnation among some of the progressive elements of society.

Second-year studies beckoned. Trang found herself looking forward with eager anticipation to seeing her friends again. Looking back to just a year earlier, she felt much more at home in her new environment and confident that her abilities matched the task ahead. But there was still another social dimension to be explored, one far beyond her experience. 'Perhaps one day,' she told herself.

Getting into the 'Swinging 60s' fashions, Sydney.

- CHAPTER 9 -

Second Year: Choices and Adaptation

Sydney, 1966

Although Trang had chosen psychology as her field of study, she did so in the knowledge that there was little or no scope for employment as a psychologist when she returned to Vietnam. The profession had yet to gain a foothold there. There was a stigma attached to mental illness, at its worst a total rejection by family and former friends lest they too be afflicted. Sufferers and their families would therefore try very hard to find a physical cause for their unwelcome feelings and behaviours. Or a spiritual consultant might be called to give them insight into the best means of dealing with the source of their illness. For these reasons, those mental health facilities that were available were typically consulted only as a last resort. Why, then, had Trang chosen that particular field of study? She explains the attraction.

> It was a new field for me, and I was fascinated by its very strong base of scientific research. I hadn't expected that. Rather, I had expected to find that the practice of psychology entailed a lot of guesswork, an element of fortune-telling if you like. But instead I found this strong scientific background and I was very much attracted to it. And especially I loved statistics and reading about all of the research studies.

Another factor in Trang's choice was that Colombo Plan scholarship holders could not avail themselves of the full range of courses on offer by their universities. Trang's preference would have been to study medicine, following in the footsteps of her elder brothers. But training in medicine at the University of Saigon was given a high priority and the institution's resources were already supplemented by foreign aid funds. It therefore wouldn't have made sense for the Colombo Plan administrators to accept Vietnamese students into medicine in donor countries. They focused instead on other areas of skill shortages like engineering and education. As well, many generalist degrees could be followed up with a Diploma of Education to provide much-needed teaching and librarianship qualifications.

As she made her subject choices, Trang did not have any particular plan for her career beyond graduation. The war was escalating and if North Vietnam prevailed it was likely that there would be no place for her in Vietnamese society. The stain of her family's relatively affluent background and previous flight from Hanoi would not be overlooked by a communist regime. One thing at a time, she decided. Concentrate on completing her undergraduate degree with good results and then reassess her situation in light of what was happening in her home country. It was not a satisfactory situation for one who was normally meticulous in her planning, but she felt there was no alternative.

Against this background of uncertainty, Trang was fortunate in her allocation of student accommodation. She stayed with the Salvation Army ladies at Marrickville throughout her undergraduate studies and beyond. She still speaks fondly of their kindness and support, attributing much of her success to them because they looked after her so well. Every morning they would bring her and Le freshly squeezed orange juice. And every night they would insist that their boarders must concentrate on completing their assignments and learning new skills instead of helping with the household chores.

The ladies clearly played a vital part in Trang's cultural adaptation, and she welcomed their wholehearted support because she was missing her family and friends so much. There were times when she longed for home, special occasions like Chinese New Year when she was reminded of traditional family celebrations. And later, when Le met her future husband and fellow student, Thai, Trang felt very, very lonely. Le and Thai did not neglect her, often taking her on outings with them, including a brief holiday in the snow country. But she still felt very much alone. And, while her time at the Salvation Army hospital had taught her much, it had done little to relieve her intense homesickness.

Trang concluded that she needed to belong in the broader community, to find something other than her studies to distract her. While she enjoyed living with the Salvation Army ladies and occasionally going to their church, she felt the urge to explore further afield, a more varied community group perhaps, people who would welcome her as one of them during her journey of discovery. Ideally she might have found a Buddhist group, but in mid-1960s Sydney Buddhism was yet to flourish. She decided to attend the local Anglican Church on Sundays with one of her close friends, whose father was a minister.

It was an engaging but ultimately disappointing experience. The Christians she met there were very kind and curious about her origins, but she was always treated as a guest, an exotic flower blown in on the wind rather than an ordinary member of the congregation. Somehow the inclusiveness just wasn't there to show that she was welcomed as an equal. She was therefore discouraged, although not resentful, as her second year of studies progressed. She wasted no time on regrets as she withdrew from her brief foray into Western religion. Interestingly, her effort to belong gives insight into a key aspect of her character. She has never been one to sit back and wait for a solution to come to her. Instead, she makes things happen, and this strength came to the fore whenever she was faced with an obstacle to acceptance in any situation. Then, if her efforts to remedy the situation failed, she would simply move on to seek a more successful solution.

Fortunately, Trang had her university friends to divert her during the academic year. This social and collegial contact ensured that her persistent feelings of homesickness and loneliness did not allow her to lapse into isolation. And, although she had to share Le from her second year onwards, Trang liked Thai. He and Le made a fine couple. They had much in common. Thai too had been born in the north, yet another whose family had fled the threat of persecution when Ho Chi Minh came to power. Like the Vu sisters, he came to Australia on a Colombo Plan scholarship. He was two years older than Le and nearing the completion of his undergraduate degree. A high-achieving student in his field of electrical engineering at the University of Sydney, Thai planned to follow up his undergraduate studies with a master's degree.

It was part way through second year that karma brought David into Trang's circle. His focus was economics, but his other studies included psychology and they met at a psychology tutorial. In second year Trang was already specialising in psychology. Her studies included a series of tutorials on psychological testing. In the course of these sessions, intelligence tests were administered to the students, a cross-section of cognitive ability assessments in which the tasks set are progressively more difficult until the subject is unable to progress further. When Trang had finished that particular tutorial, she had to rush off to a social psychology tutorial David was also attending. She had her intelligence test papers in her arms and said to him, 'I just did this test and stopped here because I can go no further.' They looked at the test together and he was promptly able to go beyond her limits. She was much impressed.

David was very bright, but also gave Trang the impression that he was shy. She had no qualms about talking to him because, in an educational environment where she was doing very well and her English was improving, she was more confident and had established her circle of Australian friends. But she took care not to get out of her depth, and this could be attributed to her own shyness. Looking back, she explains her approach to social interaction:

> I was not shy. Not really. It just depended on the environment. Maybe people thought I was shy when I arrived just because I was sitting back and keeping a low profile, trying to learn as quickly as possible. I could not enter into any detailed discussion because I was not yet really fluent. So they thought I was just shy. Actually, I think that, in the 1960s at least, people just automatically expected an Asian girl student to be quite inhibited. But many were not. And these days it is no longer an expectation. I suppose too that many Australians tended to be a little more outspoken than an Asian would be until a closer personal relationship had developed.

Whatever the case, Trang was at ease with David from the outset. By the time they moved into third year they were becoming good friends. He wasn't yet Trang's boyfriend, but the relationship showed promise of becoming closer. She was a little scared of moving too quickly, not least because she had no idea about the finer points of being in a loving relationship. In Saigon as a teenager, she hadn't been allowed to go off on dates with boys. That was how it was in her culture and she'd never as much as held hands.

As second year progressed, both on and off campus, it seemed a propitious time to grow Asian-Australian friendships. The barriers of fear and ignorance were finally breaking down. In March 1966 the new Holt government introduced much-needed changes to the White Australia policy, lowering the requirements for non-European entry, residency and citizenship. But, even as Trang welcomed this encouraging news, her anxiety about her future was growing as the Vietnam War escalated. One particularly unsettling development was the American bombing of targets in North Vietnam in a three-year operation called Rolling Thunder. Trang remembers well a psychology tutorial that discussed the bombing and its implications. It was the big news of the day, so during the tutorial all eyes were on her. The group wanted to see how she would react to the attack on her former home. The tutor even came down to her and said, 'What do you think? What do you think of the Americans bombing North Vietnam?' As Trang recalls:

> I was very upset, because my memories of North Vietnam were not about the hardship and persecution that came later. Hanoi, a beautiful city, had been my home for that early part of my life. It would be so sad if the American bombing caused widespread destruction there. I could not yet properly articulate my feelings in English, so I said little beyond how awful it was. I was surprised at the growing depth of anti-war sentiment. In the university environment many of my friends were social work students so they tended to be part of the political left. They always talked to me about the war. They would say it should not have happened, that Australians should not be there. I didn't know what to say to them, or which side I should be on. But then I received letters from Chau. She wrote that the bombing of Hanoi boosted the morale of the southern army, helping them to believe this escalation of the war effort would enable them to win. So I felt reassured that, for the people in South Vietnam, the bombing of Hanoi was a good thing if it helped to stem the communist advance.

Resolutely Trang blocked out her fears, working even harder at her studies. As the 1966 academic year moved to its close, she had already established a very strong personal and academic base for her undergraduate degree, a foundation for results that would enhance her prospects for future studies and employment. There would be much more to her life than she could have possibly foreseen and her path would not be an easy one. But for the moment there was the summer break, and with it the promise of seeing an Australian state other than New South Wales. The Salvation Army ladies were going to Melbourne for a holiday break and had offered to take Trang, Le and Tuy, a friend and fellow student who stayed with them at the Marrickville house at every opportunity. It was by far Trang's longest ever road trip, bringing home to her the huge size of the continent. The ladies drove, leaving the girls free to talk and take in the surrounding vistas. Then, at long last, the outskirts of Melbourne, a city she would come to know very well. It was also David's home. 'It was a surprise,' she remembers. 'So different from Sydney and it was cold. But we enjoyed the trip. We were tourists so we went to see everything. I remember visiting Chinatown. It was very small then and the food was horrible.'

- CHAPTER 10 -

Third Year Studies

University of New South Wales, 1967

After two years of study, Trang was expressing herself more confidently in English but still had further to go before she was satisfied with her listening proficiency.

> By third year I was immersed in psychology. David and I were still just good friends then. It was a year when we just put our heads down and studied. I can't remember much about that year at all apart from that concentration on bringing it all together. Living with the two Australian ladies and using English with them had helped me a great deal, as had my interaction with my friends at university. But listening could still be a problem. The truth is that I was still very uncomfortable when I was asked to give my input at tutorials. It wasn't the public speaking aspect. I had always been confident with that. Even as a schoolgirl, I could stand in front of a crowd and deliver material that I had prepared, and I could think on my feet so I was ready to answer questions. My difficulty was only when I was in a group and having to engage in a less structured discussion, listening to a range of opinions and then having to respond. That's when I had trouble, because I still had that difficulty in fully understanding other people.

The remnants of the language barrier aside, Trang was achieving so highly in third year that the question of an honours year inevitably arose. Dr Gault strongly encouraged her to go on because the honours year was the key to higher learning and already Trang felt a strong pull towards scientific research. And always in her mind was the question of what to do when her scholarship was completed. At the very least, she wanted to become sufficiently qualified to increase the range of options open to her. The war in Vietnam continued to escalate during 1967 and it seemed increasingly unlikely that she would be able to return to a secure life there. Fear for her family washed over her again and again, even as she resolutely tried to put thoughts of the future aside. One thing at a time, she told herself yet again. Top results were now even more important as a solid foundation for her fourth year and the pathways that might open.

As Trang concentrated on her third-year studies at UNSW, the 1960s continued its march as the decade of unprecedented challenge to the established sociocultural order. In Australia, social homogeneity was slowly giving way to the rising tide of multiculturalism. There was growing recognition that cultural diversity brought unexpected benefits, including a boost to entrepreneurialism as migrants saw opportunities to prosper through innovation and hard work.

Despite these early steps towards inclusivity, it remained a daunting experience for newcomers to adapt to a markedly different culture. Australians were masters of rough humour, cheerfully looking down upon all those who did not share their heritage as rugged individuals shaped by drought, flood, fire and war. Foreigners were commonly labelled with derogatory terms: wogs, dagoes, poms, chinks, the Yellow Peril. The use of these epithets was not always expressive of ingrained hatred, intolerance or resentment, but they were hurtful. There was however a positive side, embodied in the nation's underlying social concept of 'a fair go'. Despite the disrespect expressed freely in the casual racism of the 1960s, immigrants who worked hard and enjoyed success won increasing respect.

Trang's observations and experiences during her undergraduate years were laying the foundation for her later strong support for multiculturalism and her research into the impact of resettlement in a new land on people from very different origins. But it was another dimension to Australian society, the gender gap, she found most difficult to understand. She recalls that, when she was introduced to young female Australians during her induction period, she was often confused by their responses to her questions. She would ask, 'What are you studying at university?' or 'What is your job?' To her surprise, there seemed to be a low level of expectation and engagement.

One girl told her that she had no wish to go to university. She just wanted to be a hairdresser. Another simply said, 'I'm married,' as if that status ruled out paid work or study towards a career outside the home. It surprised her that, in many ways, the patriarchal Vietnamese society she had left behind offered more opportunities for women than were available in this Western society. It was common for Vietnamese women to manage both businesses and households. Mother was such a person. And professional careers were open to her daughters, married or not. Female participation in the workforce was not such a big deal in Saigon. There were no silly rules about healthy and intelligent married women being confined primarily to home duties. Why was it so in this place?

Fresh thoughts came to Trang every day. So much to learn, so much happening. She had no inkling then that much of her future would be inextricably bound to the issues of multiculturalism and gender equality. But it was clear to her that, in this new land, women were not valued as highly as they should be.

- CHAPTER 11 -

Trapped in Saigon

Saigon, December 1967 - March 1968

The end of the academic year came quickly, intensifying Trang's anticipation of being with her family again. Colombo Plan students were funded for one trip home during their studies. Trang had elected to take hers in late December 1967. After the flurry of preparations and farewells, she had much to reflect on during the long flight to Saigon for what was intended to be a two-week holiday. She was twenty-one and had already won respect for her excellent results in undergraduate studies. Now she was looking forward to being reunited with family and friends before returning to Sydney to complete her honours year. Surely the way ahead would be clearer by then.

As the big jet whispered north across Australia and beyond, Trang was already missing David. She knew much more about him now, and his origins in the small New South Wales country town of Tumbarumba. His family was not well off and he became determined to make a better life for himself. He left his home as a teenager, completing his secondary education in Sydney and working there to finance his university studies. Since childhood, his dream had been to become a lawyer, but he was convinced that, even if he graduated with distinction, his background was not conducive to a successful career. One needed connections to find a place as an articled clerk in an established law firm, he had told Trang. So he had decided to undertake an arts degree, majoring in psychology and economics. He was particularly attracted to the latter and now planned to follow up with postgraduate studies. He was still working part time to support himself, and he hoped that his choice of profession might at least unlock the secrets of wealth creation.

Trang was impressed by David's energy and ambition, qualities that mirrored her own determination to succeed. He had been a key element of the three undergraduate years that had broadened and enriched her life. She had indeed been fortunate and there was much to feel positive about. Why then was she sitting here, ignoring the magazine pressed into her hands by the smiling flight attendant, the joyous anticipation of arrival and reunion with her family and friends marred by her lurking conviction that there were very dark times ahead? She pushed her negative thoughts aside, knowing that she would learn much more during her visit. Her brothers Quynh and Dzi were now serving with the army as doctors, and Chau had married a colonel. They would be able to explain more about the progress of the war and what might be expected.

Her fears were temporarily forgotten in the joy and excitement of homecoming. She hugged Mother fiercely and for a while was reassured by the warmth and normality of her welcome. But it soon became apparent that Mother felt deeply pessimistic.

'What's wrong, Mother?' Trang knew but she wanted to hear her talk about it.

'It's the war,' Mother said flatly. 'I think perhaps we will lose. If that happens I don't know what we will do. I am sure of one thing. We will be treated as enemies of the state. It will be Hanoi all over again.'

Trang tried to reassure Mother, but didn't really believe her own words. There was little else to do other than busy themselves with preparations for Tet, the forthcoming Chinese New Year, in the hope that it would be an auspicious beginning to 1968. It was to be a Year of the Monkey. Monkeys were fun-loving, optimistic people, so perhaps a brighter light would shine for them in the year to come. That thought didn't work. The communist forces sought to break the deadlock by launching the 1968 Tet Offensive to coincide with the New Year celebrations, marking a new, more intensive phase of the war that would bring unprecedented suffering to the citizens of South Vietnam.

Trang was horrified by the turn of events and its implications for the safety of her family. There was also an immediate personal impact. She was trapped in Saigon indefinitely because civil air traffic in and out of the country was suspended during the offensive. More than that, experiencing the determined attack on Saigon at first hand brought a new reality to the effect of war on those around her. When she had arrived in Saigon from Australia, her cousin Kim Chi was working at the American shop, the PX, as a cashier. It was Christmas and she introduced Trang to her American and other friends. Then the offensive began and they received news that some of Kim Chi's friends were injured. Others had been captured and taken away by the Viet Cong. Trang recalls clearly her distress:

> It was a terrifying experience to be right there in the city that was the enemy's primary objective, being confronted by news that people I knew were being taken. It was then that Mother declared that it was just impossible to win the war because the enemy was everywhere. For example, there was a girl who was selling cigarettes from a little kiosk at the corner of our street. During the offensive, she was exposed as a very active Viet Cong soldier. Until then we'd just thought that here was a girl you see day by day, a very nice girl selling cigarettes. And all the time she was quite a high-ranking Viet Cong. So how would you know who is your enemy and who is your friend?

In Australia, David was becoming very concerned at the possibility that Trang might never return. There was nothing he could do except wait. But despite Mother's fears, the Tet Offensive failed to capture Saigon. The enemy backed off to regroup and flights in and out of the country were eventually allowed to resume. Trang was thus able to return to Sydney in early March 1968. Still shaken by her visit, she boarded the aircraft at Tan Son Nhat Airport with very mixed feelings. Far from shining a light on her future direction, her three years of study in Australia had been an adventure that left her trapped in uncertainty and frustration. The one saving grace was that she could continue her studies while she prayed for her family's welfare.

- CHAPTER 12 -

Honours Year

Sydney, 1968-69

The nine-hour flight from Saigon to Sydney passed slowly, Trang's mood swinging between guilt at leaving her family to face their war and the warm anticipation of being with David again. She wondered how her ancestors would regard her divided loyalties. Surely her duty was clear. She should be thinking only of her family and how she could help them. Yet another nagging voice insisted that she must also live her life, that if she could complete her education she might somehow be in a better position to help. That seemed a more rational plan. Or was she just letting herself think that because she was missing someone who had become so dear to her almost without her knowing it? She found brief solace in tears.

Her second arrival at Sydney Airport, this time not wide-eyed with curiosity but her mind seething with very different emotions. David's eyes took her in with a warmth that drew her into his arms. He was very relieved, hugging her tightly to him.

'I thought we'd lost you,' he said. 'Bloody stupid war. I hope you won't be going off over there again. What's happening with your family? Are they still safe?'

'For the present, yes. But I am very worried.'

'I'm not surprised. Media reports have been saying that the Tet Offensive was a victory for Ho's forces, that it shows they won't be beaten. In other words, South Vietnam will lose the war despite America's support. And ours. What will happen to your family then?'

'I don't know. If the worst happens, Mother will know what to do. She always does. But I'm still hoping. The war is a long way from over. I don't know why the papers are saying those things. If the offensive had been a victory for the North then I wouldn't be here now.'

Trang was still clinging to David, surprised at the strength of his feelings and even more at her own. Their relationship had somehow taken a giant leap forward while she was away. He was constantly in her thoughts during the weeks following, even as she busied herself with her honours program. After her experiences in Saigon, she felt a new resolve to prepare herself for whatever the future held. Her honours thesis would be her first significant research task, one that demanded a good result. It was indeed fortunate that she had excelled at statistics during her undergraduate program.

She saw more and more of David, daring to hope that he would share her future. He too was enamoured. Much sooner than she expected, they decided that they wanted to get married. Trang's life became quite complicated then because, when she broke the news to her family, Mother decided to fly out from Saigon. Trang was at once pleased, because she would not be here studying if not for Mother's wisdom and example, and anxious, because she needed her approval. But what if Mother concluded that David was an unsuitable match? Trang prayed that she would give her blessing. If not, she must somehow be convinced.

Mother duly arrived in September to attend the engagement gathering. She met David's parents, Arthur and Sadie, and despite the barrier of language they got along remarkably well. Both mothers were quite supportive of the proposed union. Arthur seemed uneasy but he voiced no opposition. It was hard to tell what he really thought because he was like that, a man without a lot to say. Back in Vietnam, Trang's strongly traditionalist father was of course aghast at the thought of her marrying a Westerner, and it went without saying that her brothers too would have serious misgivings. Trang's commitment to David was such a big thing for her family that she supposed they were all still trying to take it in. She could almost hear them lamenting her waywardness. 'That's what comes of young girls running off to another country to study instead of trusting their parents to find suitable matches. They lose their sense of what's right.' But none of them were in Sydney to raise objections and Mother didn't say much about their views.

It was just after the engagement that unforeseen complications arose. Mother became ill with a kidney infection, so ill that she was hospitalised for treatment for several months. Trang was worried sick and, when added to the pressure of completing her honours thesis, it was a very difficult time for her. David was his usual supportive self but there was little he could do to help. It was her supervisor and mentor, Dr Una Gault, who gave her the caring encouragement and support that only another woman could provide. Fortunately, Trang had chosen her honours thesis well. Her topic was repression, about how people repress unpleasant memories. It was a very interesting and unusual thesis, a testing of Freudian theory that was ideally suited to her skills in applied statistics.

The end of 1968 brought another key family development. With Mother's support during her convalescence, Le and Thai had made their decision to settle in Canada instead of trying to return to Vietnam to start a new life there. Le recalls the occasion:

> It was Mother's idea, actually. She knew of another Vietnamese student who had completed his PhD studies in Australia. He had taken his family to Canada for the same reasons. So we followed in their footsteps. We applied to the Canadian High Commission in Sydney. We were accepted right away, because in those days the Canadian government was very open to immigration. They had a points system. If you met their criteria, they would accept you. And they needed young professional people, speaking English or French, preferably both. So we had no problems being accepted.

Mother left in early 1969 with Thai and Le. So it all turned out well enough and, although Trang would miss Le very much, she was still very happy because Mother, in fact all of the female side of her family, had accepted her engagement. She thought that it was quite ironic that her father and her brothers still did not share that enthusiasm. She wondered if they realised that, if the situation was reversed, so many Australians would hold the same view for essentially the same reasons. Mixed marriages were socially undesirable and doomed to fail.

Meanwhile, as she completed her thesis, Trang's confidence was reinforced by her research results. She had used very sophisticated statistical analysis to support her findings and was rewarded with first-class honours. She was the first Asian woman to graduate with a first in Psychology from

UNSW. And already it was time to think of the next step towards a career that would transform her from the eighth and least important child in her family to one who had shown that she had the same potential as any of her siblings.

Left: Trang and David defy convention to become engaged, Sydney, 1968.

Above: Mentor Dr Una Gault, UNSW, celebrates Trang's engagement.

Trang's mother meets Trang's future mother-in-law Sadie Thomas. Sydney, 1968.

- CHAPTER 13 -

Marriage

Sydney, 1969-70

Undaunted by the lack of paternal enthusiasm for their union, Trang and David decided to set a wedding date in May 1969. The big day would be just after her graduation from honours year. It was not feasible to arrange a traditional Vietnamese wedding, of course. Trang's family would not be there and she knew only a handful of Vietnamese students who might swell the numbers on her side. She and David were free to choose whatever they wished by way of ceremony, so why not an Australian wedding?

That decision made, the choice of venue and celebrant was not as simple. Even in the late 1960s, who one married and where the union was solemnised was a serious business for most Australians. As an ethnic Vietnamese raised in the Buddhist tradition and now entering into marriage with a Christian man from a different culture, Trang anticipated at least minor issues in the choice of an appropriate venue. She was right. David's own religious background was mixed. His mother was Anglican, while his father was from a very strongly Methodist family who had wanted David's mother to convert. Undeterred, she married him anyway, and eventually the three children of the marriage were baptised into the Anglican Church.

Given this background, Trang and David's first consultation when planning their wedding was with the local Anglican minister. This gentleman was not enthused, refusing to marry the happy couple unless Trang first converted to the Anglican faith. She agreed to think about it. Their next port of call was the Wesley Chapel at Sydney University, where David was now enrolled in postgraduate studies in economics. David's parents had no issues with that idea, as they weren't insistent that David should follow the

Anglican path. The minister at the Wesley Chapel was a younger, friendlier cleric. 'We'll marry you here,' he responded cheerfully. 'No worries.'

There was another, much more personal aspect of wedding preparations that took Trang into unknown territory. She was totally uneducated about physical intimacy. In Saigon, there was no such thing as sex education at school. She recalls that, during her Year 12 studies, class members were tasked to write an essay on the topic of 'My Best Friend'. One of her more creative classmates wrote an essay about a fictional friend whom she suspected of being homosexual. The teacher was beside herself. 'Oh, where did you hear such a wicked word? You are an evil girl!'

So it was that, when Trang left for Australia at eighteen, she had never been allowed to mix with boys. Sex was a strictly taboo subject, a matter just not discussed in the home.

'I didn't know exactly how children were made, not even the example of the birds and the bees,' she laughs. 'And even when I met David in second year I was still quite uneducated.'

By then Trang had Australian male friends other than David. Some of them would come to the house in Marrickville to study with her. They would ask her to help with problem-solving and how she approached particular assignments. They borrowed her research reports to help them with their own. It never occurred to Trang that these friendships could lead to something more.

'They knew that I was a serious student,' she says, 'not the kind of girl to be asked out to a movie, that sort of thing. So the interaction was always about whether they could have a look at my work, get a copy of my research report before I handed it in. No boy ever asked me out or anything beyond that.'

To the experienced and more cynical outsider, it is not surprising that these young men were less interested in Trang as a person than as a prized source of free information and assistance. Expediency is ever the enemy of conscience. It was therefore not until she met David in second year that she began to feel any interest in a deeper friendship. Even then, there was nothing sudden about it. Her interest in him as a male didn't really develop until the beginning of the third year when, by chance, they were both members of a group of four students involved in a social psychology project.

They saw more of each other as a consequence, and again by chance had a mutual close friend in the group who encouraged David to ask Trang out to a movie while also encouraging Trang to go to the movies more often. Their devious friend also took it upon herself to tell Trang a little about sex.

'I wasn't interested,' Trang recalls. 'And when we began to date David also did not push me. He was going through a period in which he was a romantic, gentlemanly type. The furthest he went was to take my hand at the movies and hold it. And we never went beyond that.'

For the times, that was a fairly cautious approach to a relationship. Even after their decision to marry, she and David still hadn't progressed beyond kissing and holding hands. Fortunately, Trang's girlfriends advised her to 'see about getting checked out to make sure that, you know, everything is in place and working. And you should go on the Pill if you don't want to start a family straight away.' One of them recommended a gynaecologist she knew who would prescribe the necessary contraceptive and check Trang out physically to make sure she was a healthy, normal young lady. Some women still had reservations about the Pill and what side effects it might have, so a gynaecologist would make sure that she had all the right information.

Trang duly made the appointment, which was very expensive as she had no health insurance. The gynaecologist turned out to be an older man, very experienced and caring. He conducted a physical examination and everything was in order. But he was so surprised at her lack of knowledge that he volunteered some hints on what to do and not to do when it came to physical intimacy. 'You are a very, very nice girl,' he told her. 'So my fee is my wedding present to you.'

Trang was astonished and grateful for his caring and generous attitude, the last thing she expected from someone she'd never seen before. 'But then,' she smiles, 'he'd never run across a young woman of twenty-three who was so ignorant of conjugal matters. David too was so caring. He did not try to take over the role of educating me. He didn't push me along even after we were married. He just accepted that I was learning in my own way.'

The marriage duly proceeded. Some fifty relatives and guests, the latter mostly fellow students, attended the service. Trang's elder sister Dung came to visit from Saigon, arriving just before the big day. David's mother, Sadie, was very supportive. More than that, she was very happy, having long since wished for a daughter of her own. A strong and straightforward woman, in many ways she reminded Trang of Mother. Both had enjoyed their meeting at the engagement celebration. But Arthur, a reticent man indeed, still showed no particular emotion. Trang always felt that her father-in-law was bewildered about her. She supposed that a lot of people, especially men, could not understand why some of their sons were fighting the Vietnamese while others were marrying their young women. Perhaps, to them, it was a somehow un-Australian thing to do.

The wedding guests too had varying opinions regarding the suitability of their match, and despite Trang's happiness this added, at least for her, an element of cultural tension. In the lead-up to the occasion, quite a number of their friends were much less concerned about the religious aspects of David and Trang's union than its status as a mixed marriage. When the couple had announced their engagement, Trang's girlfriends, some of whom were looking forward to their own weddings, had been very supportive. As Trang explains:

> For some reason, honours year is the year of getting married, so I had many girlfriends also taking the long step to a permanent relationship. We were all very happy as we discussed our wedding preparations, talking up the virtues of our boyfriends and anticipating the lasting joy we would bring them. On the other hand, there were concerns among our male counterparts. Many of David's friends had been quite surprised that he wished to marry me. He was tall and blond, you see. And his very close friends, who knew him long before we met, also knew what his previous girlfriends had looked like. They were tall and blond and very Australian. So his friends could not understand. I just did not fit the mould of his usual girlfriends. And actually, several of them said to him that it would not last and tried to talk him out of it. All of this just because I was different.

The other thing that had ruffled Trang's feathers was that, ever since she and David had become close, some of his friends had been condescending towards her. She had gained the impression that they saw themselves as upper-class, quite sophisticated types who apparently thought of her as just coming out of the jungle. Their cross-cultural understanding was very poor. They assumed that she knew little, especially about their concept of culture. She recalls one of his friends sitting down to talk to her about opera. 'You know opera?' he asked. 'They tell the stories by singing songs. Good singers, too.' And it wasn't just the men. Some of her Australian girlfriends were determined to educate her; for example, by explaining the plots of movies and their significance. But she found it hard to take offence at well-meaning attempts to educate her in Western culture. She felt it wasn't so much prejudice as ignorance. By and large, Asians were regarded as peasants from agricultural villages. And peasant women had their babies in the rice paddies and then got on with their work of planting and harvesting. That was the popular image. There was nothing consciously derogatory in the attempts by their friends, male or female, to explain customs and institutions they assumed were unique to the West. Yet she felt resentful at times because it was these assumed differences that made it more challenging for her to adapt to her new life. Paradoxically, she feels that she also derived a benefit from her experiences.

> I think that this issue became another reason underlying my determination to succeed. Perhaps I was driven just a little, not only by my innate ambition, but also because I wanted to show these people that I was not just some little girl out of the jungle or the village. I enjoyed proving people wrong, and watching their surprise.

That said, it is evident now that Trang's drive to succeed was much more broadly based. To her, the desire to achieve is just another human trait. It is natural to go on studying and, when you achieve, to keep on achieving highly when you proceed to your choice of career. In her case, the idea of that progression was reinforced by the influence that Mother had over all of the children. Her marriage to David was another step away from self-doubt, one that made her feel more optimistic about the future. She now had someone to share her life, to make her feel that she belonged and was loved for the woman she was rather than a curiosity, a bright but temporary part of the student group.

There was time for a brief honeymoon in Canberra to see the sights of the national capital before she and David returned to their studies with keen anticipation of the years to come. She had learned the basics of love and marriage, enough to know she had much more to learn. Typically, she decided that, over the years to come, she would educate herself thoroughly about sex and gender relationships. So at an opportune time she took herself off to see a practitioner, Dr Elsie Koadlow, who was known for helping women who were lacking in such knowledge. As Trang recalls:

> She was much older than me, really one of a kind. And she was just so good. She taught people like me to be comfortable with their anatomy. And long before I saw her, in fact soon after we were married, I started to buy novels, really sexy novels. And the funny thing about it was that, for me, learning about relationships was no big deal. As I went on with my psychology career, I read a lot of the research by Masters and Johnson, the first researchers to do a lot about male and female sexual responses. Years later, at RMIT University, when the Psychology Department felt there should be a course to teach the students about the psychology of sex, I had learned so much that I volunteered to teach the course.
>
> I called it the Psychology of Gender. In the first few lectures we would talk about gender differences, men and women in society, quite a lot of scientific stuff. But one of the lectures was about the differences in anatomy. I'd discuss with them the ground-breaking research by Masters and Johnson in the 1970s, about how men and women respond differently. I taught all that and my course was just so popular. And, as you know, it was my practice to tell a joke every fifteen minutes or so. So I told sexual jokes, and the kids just could not believe that I would do that. I'd do it with a straight face and you could hear a pin drop. Students who were doing other courses would come to listen in. So many told me years later that they could not believe I would give such lectures with a straight face. And I would tell them I could do it because it was just not a great big deal for me. I just wasn't shy about the subject, or embarrassed by talking about it. It's all part of the science. Except for the jokes, of course. The really funny part about it was that I was the only one who would give those lectures.

That experience was of course well in the future as Trang worked hard to complete her master's degree, a consolidation of the skills she had thus far developed with distinction. But it illustrates very clearly the determination and adaptability that were already inherent in her approach to each new stage of her life. 'It's not such a big deal' was a guiding principle that would serve her well in the decades ahead.

Salvation Army ladies, Mrs Jeffries and Miss Gale, join Trang and her sister Dung to celebrate her high academic achievement in 1969. The first Asian female student to graduate from UNSW with First Class Honours.

Trang weds David at the Wesley Chapel, University of Sydney, 10 May, 1969.

- CHAPTER 14 -

Postgraduate Studies

Macquarie University, Sydney, 1969-70

Trang and David's wedding, in May 1969, had taken place in the context of another crowded academic year. They were both undertaking their master's programs. Trang had been accepted at Macquarie University. David was studying part time at Sydney University while working part time in the Research Department at the Reserve Bank of Australia. It was his first serious job. 'One of the great virtues of working at the RBA,' he would say, 'is that one learns a great deal about money very quickly.' Shortly afterwards they bought a block of land, intending to build a house when they had completed their studies and could afford the leap from rented accommodation to their own home.

Trang's thesis was on conformity in adolescents, conformity in same-sex and mixed groups, and conformity to authority. She describes it as very much a classic research experiment. Data collection entailed putting individuals of both genders into various situations to quantify the extent to which their responses conformed. For example, Trang would create a classic test situation in which one boy's responses to questions about a picture were compared with those of a group of five other boys. The questions sought factual responses, right or wrong. For example, how long is a line and is it longer than another line? The group members would be primed beforehand to give, one by one, a deliberately wrong answer to see how the single boy reacted. Some subjects would disagree, but others would conform to the group's response. Variations on the test included permutations and combinations such as opposite-sex peer groups and whether or not the participation of an authority figure influenced the subject's responses. Trang recalls:

> I went to all these schools, co-ed schools, gender-specific schools, and for the authority figures I would get the school principals to sit in. And the kids would be thinking, 'How could a school principal get something so obviously wrong? How can I disagree with him?' It was very interesting research and I must say that I had strong support from my supervisor at Macquarie, John Collins. John had been a teacher in his first career and therefore had a lot of contacts. So it was just a matter of approaching these different schools. Some would agree, some would not. And, once a principal agreed to help, then he could get the teachers on side. For my part, I would try not to interrupt classes too much. They would let the kids out into a separate room so that I could conduct the experiments.

Reflecting on her time at Macquarie as a postgraduate student, Trang explains that the university was then in its very first years.

> So in its way, it was a very nice community to study in. I remember that there were only about thirty overseas students. And I was the only Vietnamese. The staff looked out for our welfare very well, a lot of care, a lot of attention. It was such a close-knit community that I remember walking along and seeing the Vice-Chancellor and he would call out my name. That sort of thing would never happen now. And in those days, postgraduate students each had an office. There were just a few of us and it was such a huge campus, all of the new buildings.

She recalls that the staff had much trouble with her name. Her Vietnamese name was four words, Vu Thi Ngoc Trang. She would explain that her surname was Vu, but no one seemed to understand the different naming convention. After her marriage in May, only about three months into her studies, she came back to her office to find that her name had already been changed. It was now Trang Thomas. Nobody had asked her. The staff had just assumed that she would take David's surname. They were very pleased with themselves for simplifying her title. 'It would not have happened ten years later,' says Trang. 'By then it was becoming more acceptable for women to keep their own name.'

The change of name was not the only assumption that was made about her marriage. One of her teachers back home in Vietnam was a

Catholic priest. She'd kept in touch with some of her old friends and her schoolteachers. The priest not only assumed she would take David's name but also took it for granted that because David was a Christian, his level of commitment would be as high as that of the Catholics in Vietnam. Trang would naturally enter into his faith. So he sent Trang a card saying 'Welcome to the Christian family.'

Trang took no offence. It was not a big deal to her to be identified as David's dutiful wife. More importantly, she was working very hard to complete her thesis as quickly as possible because she and David had plans to travel before committing themselves to the next phase of their lives. She submitted her paper in August 1970. Her results, which once again gained her honours, were published in a journal article and later as two chapters in a book on the topic of conformity in young people.

David, too, completed his studies quickly, then took a year's leave of absence from his job at the Reserve Bank so he and Trang could set off on their first grand adventure, an extended overseas trip to England via Singapore, Malaysia, Vietnam, Thailand, Laos, Burma (now Myanmar) and onwards through Afghanistan, Iran and Iraq. In 1970 it was possible to travel freely through countries that are much less accessible now. It promised to be a very engrossing and enjoyable trip, not least because it was a dream honeymoon as well. The year since their marriage had been different and reassuring, a period of acceptance when Trang no longer encountered veiled references to the likely duration of mixed marriages. They were moving in different circles by then. It helped that David's friends had also graduated and scattered to various locations. It had been a year of hard work, concentration and mutual discovery, and now it was time to reap the first material rewards of their diligence.

- CHAPTER 15 -

First Taste of Travel

Around the world, 1970-71

Trang and David's celebratory journey offered a welcome opportunity to visit Trang's family in Saigon. Despite the Allied nations' inability to win the war, Saigon was still in South Vietnamese hands and Tan Son Nhat Airport was open for business. David was as keen as Trang to meet the rest of her family in the hope that he might now be accepted as a suitable husband. It was a fruitful visit. He did and said all the right things, trying hard to communicate in his rudimentary Vietnamese. He mastered chopsticks and the rite of obeisance. First son Phuong was by now quite supportive, and his influence in the family helped very much to promote David's acceptance. Trang was so proud of her new husband and too happy to be overly concerned by her father's unspoken but stubborn disapproval. They had not been close as she grew up and nothing had really changed now that she was an adult.

Trang had been granted Australian citizenship after completing her master's program. Looking forward immensely to life in her new land, she was pleased and proud to be carrying her Australian passport. The pair spent several months getting to London from Vietnam, travelling via the Middle East and greatly enjoying the experience. One of the joys of travel for Trang was that she already had friends she could catch up with, fellow boarders at Marrickville who had undertaken shorter study programs and since returned to South-East Asia. She recalls that English language skills were a great asset for prospective brides in Malaysia. Families who could afford the fees would send their daughters to Australia for a year or two to further their education and study the language.

I had this girlfriend who had also boarded with the Salvation Army ladies. She was absolutely beautiful, extremely elegant. When she finished her studies she went home and got married to the eighth or ninth son of one of the richest men in the country. Later, when David and I went there and visited her, we stayed at her house. Her situation was most interesting. I should first explain that, in Australia, I had been surprised to find that it was quite a scandalous thing for wealthy men to have mistresses. In South-East Asian countries it was generally accepted and indeed expected. My friend - I'll call her Jane - told me about her father-in-law, and how he had mistresses in many places that he travelled to regularly. Not just in Malaysia, but in Hong Kong, Singapore, wherever. He had children with them, and each time a mistress gave him a son he would buy her a Rolls-Royce. His whole family knew about it. It was no big deal. Some of the mistresses were the same ages as his daughters. Still no big deal. So when Jane married into this family, she understood that one day it would be like that for her. And, when we visited her, we didn't see her husband at all. If he wasn't off somewhere on business, he'd be in a nightclub or wherever with his mistresses. She stayed home with her two children, servants galore, nannies and a bodyguard. I don't know whether the bodyguard was to keep her safe or to make sure that she didn't go out and get into any mischief. So she led this really quiet life, spending her nights listening to music on her own. I don't really know if she was happy or not. She just accepted her lot.

It didn't always turn out that way, of course. I had a second friend, Rose, who'd boarded with us and the same fate befell her. But she was a much more modern girl, especially after being educated in Australia. And she just wouldn't accept that it was okay for her husband to have a mistress. So they were divorced. They had three children, so he gave her lots of money to have her own house and raise them in wealthy circumstances. David and I visited her as well. We had a great time as she let us have her Mercedes and chauffeur to see the sights. She was clearly well supported, well off. So that's the story of two different women in an Asian culture.

Those experiences brought to mind my own cultural background. I grew up amid all these families in which the husband would have a second and even a third wife. It was very common and, as in Jane's case, it was no big deal. For example, the father of one of my friends married two sisters. Now, the two sisters were very close, so they ganged up on him and bossed him around. Gave him a really hard time. So stories about men having two or more 'wives' is no surprise for me. We had adopted the French rule of law, under which only one wife is permitted. So the extra wives were in fact mistresses, concubines, whatever. They were just called wives because they were much more than mistresses. A wealthy man might set them up in a different house. If not, they would live in the same house with his legal wife and work out matters of status among themselves. Often the first wife controls and runs the family business, so she has a lot of power. She will also be responsible for the children and their education. The second wife will probably be responsible for running the household, the kitchen, domestic things in general. So they'll work it out. Sometimes they'll get along extremely well. Sometimes the second wife will just know her place and act accordingly. Having ten or twelve kids in the family is quite common. Now, the point of this whole story is that it's just not a big issue like it is in Australia. The Western culture just puts so much emphasis on monogamy. A man can have sexual relations with only one woman. However, I must add that my mother was, like Rose, a very modern woman. She would never have put up with my father having a second wife. But she was the exception, not the rule.

After their interlude in Malaysia, an engaging cultural awareness lesson for David, the happy couple resumed their journey. On their arrival in London, David was lucky enough to get a temporary job in the Australian Reserve Bank office there, with unexpected benefits. 'It's a great salary,' he told Trang. 'And I don't have to pay income tax. I don't understand why, but I'm not going to argue too much about it.'

It was winter by then, so David's job filled in the months when touring was a poor option. More importantly, he made enough money to meet their expenses for the rest of their year of travel. During the days, Trang spent much of her time in the local library. It was very cold and the library was the only place that had free heating so she was happy to indulge her love of learning while waiting for the joys of spring and further adventure. The break also gave her ample time to relax and reflect. So much had happened during the six years since she had stepped off the aircraft in Sydney, a teenager in the grip of intense homesickness. She felt now that karma must have been with her or she would not be here in London, seeing the world with her very clever husband.

In May 1971, the warmth of impending summer saw Trang and David backpacking around Europe: the UK, France, Belgium, Luxembourg, Italy, Greece, Russia and Scandinavia. It was a leisurely, carefree exploration of different lands and cultures, a journey they enjoyed to the fullest before returning to Sydney via the USA, Canada, Mexico and Fiji. They had bought relatively cheap round-trip airline tickets with the condition that they kept travelling in the same direction. Their world trip was a profound experience for both of them, and they knew then that travel would be an important part of their lives if circumstances permitted. For Trang, the absorption lay in the cultural diversity as well as the sheer beauty of the world.

> Europe was so different from my native Vietnam and Australia. I couldn't get enough of it to make even a dent in my insatiable curiosity. And it made me believe that, despite the horrendous conflicts of the twentieth century, there was a strong undercurrent of desire among most peoples to live in harmony. I decided then that I wanted to make some sort of contribution to that goal.

They arrived back to Sydney in time for David to resume his job with the RBA after his year of absence. Meanwhile, Trang began to look for employment.

> Someone said to me - I forget who - that there was a research assistant job at Macquarie. So I went there and got the job. I worked for a lecturer in education. He went to New Guinea, collecting lots of data about New Guinean students. He brought it back and I just used my statistics skills to analyse it for him. I wrote it up and that suited him very well. When I left he wrote me a very nice reference saying that I was the best research assistant he'd ever had. So that was my first job,

the first small step into my academic career.

It was at this time too that Trang and David began to give serious thought to their longer term future. They still had the block of land they had bought in anticipation of building in Sydney. But somehow that goal had morphed into a grand plan to go to the country and have a farm, still as academics. It was fashionable in the 1970s to want to be different and they had seen at first hand the many attractions of rural life during their travels. Coincidentally, it was a time of rapid expansion in Australia's tertiary education sector, so there were new opportunities for employment in regional areas. Later that year, a recruitment drive for the Riverina College of Advanced Education (CAE), now Charles Sturt University, was conducted in Sydney. Trang and David applied successfully to join the institution, not in specific appointments at that time but on the understanding that appointments appropriate to their qualifications and experience would be offered on arrival. That major step in their plan achieved, they prepared to depart the familiar environs of Sydney for the provincial city of Wagga Wagga.

'This is it.' David smiled as they set off. He waved his hand at the vast expanse of forest stretching to the smoky blue hills in the distance. 'This is the real Australia. This is what we call the Bush.'

It was a wonderful day, and as it drew on Trang began to get a better sense of the true immensity and emptiness of the land she now called home. Apart from her trip to Melbourne with the Salvation Army ladies, this was her longest venture outside Sydney by road. Then they turned off the Bruce Highway to head for Wagga Wagga, stopping a few kilometres later at a roadside service station for fuel and lunch. Trang went out for a while to look around and when she joined David again she said, 'It's really the wide open spaces here, isn't it?'

David realised at once that she'd been thinking about the prospect of life in what Australians fondly called 'the middle of nowhere' or 'beyond the black stump'.

> Something in her voice alerted me to her sense of displacement. As we drove off, I said quietly that maybe our plan wasn't going to work. And that was about the end of the farm idea. Not well thought through at all. We should have at least tried living in the country before we

embarked on our plan. However, we were committed to the shift to Wagga Wagga. We either worked at the college or we were unemployed.

In her homeland, it would have been the thing to do for Trang to consult an expert, someone like her father, before making such a life-changing decision as a move from city to country. That might well have put paid to any thought of leaving the familiar environs of Sydney and its academic institutions. But, as David said, the die was cast and soon after they arrived in Wagga Wagga. It was the beginning of an experience that Trang would have much preferred not to have had.

First taste of travel. Trang and David take in the Himalayan vista en route to Europe, 1970.

- CHAPTER 16 -

Discrimination

Riverina College of Advanced Education, Wagga Wagga, 1972

After five successful years of study and the excitement of marriage and travel, it was at the Riverina CAE that Trang encountered the first major cultural and gender obstacles to her professional advancement. Her move to the college was a pivotal experience, the marker where the hard yards of being a woman climbing through the academic ranks began.

She presented herself at the CAE, quietly proud of the fresh MA (Hons) after her name and her stint as a research assistant at Macquarie University to attest to her standing at that institution. She was shocked and disappointed when, instead of the lecturer position she had anticipated, she was offered an appointment as assistant lecturer. For the first time, her expectations and hopes were dashed. She found it hard to cope with the setback, especially when David was appointed to a senior lecturer position. Unlike Trang, he had not achieved honours in either of his degrees. On the other hand, his experience as a research economist with the RBA would have been a key factor. Trang swallowed her pride and accepted the position of assistant lecturer because she wanted to work and she felt sure that her qualifications would soon lead to promotion. That was not to be. Further, she found that what was happening to her was not an isolated case.

> In those days, because Wagga Wagga was in the country, a lot of people went there to work as couples. As in our case, sometimes the wives would be just as qualified as the husbands, or even more so, but despite that the CAE thought that they could get the wives for very low salaries. The thinking was that the wives had little choice, that they were just following their husbands. So the husbands got the good jobs

and the wives were offered what was left. It was like getting two birds for the price of one. One of the wives, fully qualified with a university degree, was offered a job as a secretary. And she was willing to take it rather than being unemployed.

Not all of the women accepted their lot. Some refused, preferring to be at home rather than being paid at very low levels. When Trang accepted and joined the Psychology Department as an assistant lecturer, she found that her nominal duties were actually those of a tutor. The position had been designated as assistant lecturer simply because that sounded more prestigious. The real sting was that she was expected to lecture, even though she was being paid well below the lecturer level. The situation she was in would not be tolerated today, but in the early 1970s new institutions were not always governed by the rules of fair play. Trang was still unable to understand why she was being treated so poorly. Her qualifications were so impressive, outranked only by a PhD. And, in those days, comparatively few lecturers had attained that level. 'I was still so naive,' she says, 'that I went along with what was happening in the belief that my skills were being tested before a better offer was forthcoming.'

Far from improving, Trang's situation worsened. It transpired that her position was under an American lecturer who had no qualifications in psychology. His PhD was in philosophy, but he was head of the Psychology Department. There was another woman there who had an honours degree in psychology, but she too was only an assistant lecturer. So the two women did all of the teaching because they were the ones who were qualified. Trang still shakes her head in disbelief.

> The guy in charge of us actually had a nervous breakdown and finished up in hospital. He was supposed to be teaching but didn't have the knowledge. It just goes to show how powerful the people at the top could be in those days. They just didn't care. And there wasn't a union to represent staff interests or even a staff association then. So for that year, I was really frustrated. I just felt that my job was far below my qualifications. And it was no consolation that other women received the same treatment. I was disappointed because I just didn't feel accepted as someone who had something fresh and exciting to offer. Instead I

> felt unwanted and unimportant, as if I was once again the eighth child and a girl at that.

It was Trang's first real taste of discrimination, coincidentally at a time when the rising tide of feminist activism was sweeping the country. She would learn much more about this movement in the years ahead, but didn't need to rely on its impetus. Even in the early 1970s she was not one to let the injustice of her treatment go unchallenged. She protested and the matter went as far as the Vice-Chancellor, who informed her that her accent was a major stumbling block. She was outraged. After years of struggling to understand lecturers who did not realise their communication skills were wanting, this arrogant man was telling Trang that her carefully expressed English was not good enough. They had quite a strong exchange of words and it was then she decided she would not stay for the following year. Instead, she would have to look for other opportunities. She also decided that, if ever she rose to a position of influence, she would present a paper on the communications gap between Australian lecturers and students from non-English-speaking backgrounds.

Despite her anger, Trang determined that she would take full advantage of her assistant lecturer position to further develop her knowledge and presentation skills.

> My vocabulary was still not very extensive, so I could not waffle. Instead I wrote down very clearly every point that I made. I worked very hard, reading up on all of the techniques. And I was also careful, while I was lecturing, to break up the serious points with a joke. I've done that ever since. It lightens up the atmosphere, and the students like it. They said I was the best. But, even though my students supported me, saying that I was the best lecturer, it was clear that I could not make any progress. I tried many times during that year. It was a strange time. One of the men in a position of authority actually said to me: 'David has such a good job. What would you do with the extra money? Even if we give you more money there is nothing in Wagga to spend it on.' I really had to go, otherwise I would just get angrier. So I applied for a lecturer position for the following year at the Gippsland Institute of Advanced Education, located at Morwell in Victoria. The Institute offered me not

just a lectureship, but placed me halfway up the seniority levels. So I showed the offer to the people at Riverina. I told them I was prepared to leave my husband to go down there to work. But they didn't believe I would leave without David.

Trang was not the only one to leave. She recalls that the end of the 1972 academic year saw an exodus of female staff. Some, like her, applied for positions elsewhere. Others decided to stay at home. It was clear that the Riverina CAE staffing model for women was broken.

David was very supportive of her stand despite the obvious difficulties of their impending separation. In early 1973, it was with conflicting feelings of sadness and keen anticipation that Trang left Wagga to take on her new challenges at the Gippsland Institute. She would not have David's comforting presence constantly at hand, and that meant living on her own for the first time in her life. A new job, new surroundings, new friends to make. She vowed she would gain as much as possible from the experience to make the sacrifice of leaving David behind worthwhile.

Years afterwards, Trang realised that her unpleasant time at Wagga was in many ways fortunate because it completely changed her attitude and, eventually, her life. As a woman whose academic career almost failed in its first full year, she became determined to achieve highly just to show her detractors that she was not the type to stay in an untenable situation simply because she had a successful husband. She now believes that, without the spur of that painful and belittling experience, she would probably have been content to have a medium-level career as a lecturer, take whatever time off was necessary to look after the children when they arrived and be content with her achievements.

- CHAPTER 17 -

Fresh Start

Morwell, Victoria, 1973-74

Trang's year of travail at Wagga had also seen the end of the Allied forces' involvement in the Vietnam War. It had long been evident that the conflict could not be won other than by massive destruction of infrastructure and the civilian population, a reversion to the 'brute force' prosecution of the Great Wars. It was equally clear that such a victory would achieve little other than perpetual guilt for the victors and the strengthening of anti-American sentiment internationally. Finally, it would entail a hugely dangerous escalation of the Cold War. Given these factors, the only sensible option was to withdraw. As the Allies departed, the South Vietnamese Army continued alone in its resistance to the North's numerically superior forces. It fought well in the face of diminishing supplies and troops, but the struggle was already a lost cause.

During her trip to Morwell, with her bridges to Riverina CAE well and truly burned, Trang's thoughts had turned increasingly to her family in Saigon while the United States and Australia repatriated their forces. She thought often of her cousin Kim Chi in those days. Kim Chi had married the previous year, in Saigon, but Trang had been unable to attend her wedding. Now the news had come that Kim Chi's mother had passed away, sad tidings tempered only by relief that Kim Chi had a husband to share her sorrow and support her through her bereavement.

Trang and her cousin had been very close since their childhood in Hanoi, when Kim Chi and her mother had joined the Vu household. Theirs was a very sad story. Kim Chi was born in 1942, shortly before the Japanese occupation of Vietnam during World War II. Her father was appointed as

Ambassador to Japan. He never returned, and did not communicate with Kim Chi's mother. Trang's parents took them in. Trang, her sister Le and Kim Chi grew up together, constant companions.

When Trang and her family left the north after Ho's victory against the French, Kim Chi and her mother elected to come to Saigon as well. So their close relationship continued until the end of high school, when Kim Chi left to work with her mother. Now she was married to an army officer and Trang worried because, after losing her father before she even knew him, and now her mother, it would be tragic if she lost her husband as well in the war.

Trang worried too about her sister Kim, who had looked after her siblings so well during those early months in Saigon before their parents arrived from the north. Kim was thirteen years Trang's elder. By the time Trang left Saigon in 1964 she was married with two children, and had graduated as a pharmacist in 1961. Now, in 1972, there were four young children and, although Kim and her husband were doing well, it would be difficult for them to move quickly in the event of a communist victory. In far-off Australia, there was little that Trang could do other than keep monitoring the progress of the war and praying for her family's safety. She hated what was happening to her former home and the constant threat to her loved ones. The prospect of the fall of South Vietnam was strengthening daily, as menacing as the looming, slow-moving storm fronts that rolled across the Australian landscape. She was grateful for David's support. He'd been there and he understood the situation very well, just as he understood that she had to move on from the Riverina CAE.

Even as she went through the business of new accommodation and initial contact in Morwell, the constant distraction of thoughts of her family persisted and strengthened. At times, as she ate her solitary dinner, she could think of little else. It was an unsettling and frustrating time, as much due to her new loneliness as her family's uncertain future. 'At least, she told herself, 'I will be earning more here, and that will put me into a better position to help them when the time inevitably comes for them to flee their homes once more.' In the meantime, she had to try to focus on the task at hand. And, as if to reward her for taking her stand at Wagga, it was soon evident that her luck had changed. At the Gippsland IAE, Trang was delighted to find that she was treated very differently from the way she had been expected to take second or third best and like it at the Riverina College.

> They really valued me at Morwell. I was put in charge of second year as a psychology lecturer. It was a very small department, only three or four of us, but totally different from the one I'd just left. And there was a new dimension. I met and worked with a number of women who were in their various ways quite strongly feminist. So I learned quite a lot more about women's rights and the issues of equality that the feminist movement was pursuing so strongly. Until then, my strengths really came from Mother. She was my role model. I hadn't known anything much about Germaine Greer or the broader women's movement or the full extent of discrimination until that year while I was living on my own, mixing with these women professionally and socially. And after experiencing discrimination myself I was ready to learn. There was one woman who was a sociologist and extremely strong in her feminist views. So I learned quite a lot from her about the systemic discrimination that women were experiencing.

Despite the dimensions of the feminist struggle, there was at least some encouraging progress. By 1973, substantial reforms were advancing the cause of equal opportunity for women. The Equal Pay Case of 1972 had established the principle of equal pay for equal work, with equal pay for women to be phased in by 1975. Women working in the Commonwealth Public Service were granted maternity leave entitlements. The Women's Electoral Lobby had been established with the aim of increasing women's influence over election participation and outcomes, and Elizabeth Reid was appointed as the first adviser to the prime minister on women's affairs. On the welfare side, a new Supporting Mother's Benefit was established for deserted wives. These were very welcome advances, giving women everywhere much to discuss and plan in their push for further reforms.

While she was very happy in her new position, Trang missed David constantly. There was, however, a brighter side. David's parents now lived in Melbourne. She and David met there at every opportunity - public holidays and term breaks - managing to get together about once a month. Then there was more good news. David received a scholarship to study for his

PhD at Monash University in Melbourne, commencing in 1974. It was a very important step in his career progress, indeed essential for an ambitious academic. He applied for and was granted leave of absence from the Riverina CAE. It was also to be a very fulfilling time for him, a time when he at last felt that he was working in a truly academic atmosphere.

The most important event of all came in August 1973. Trang became pregnant, with the baby expected in May 1974. Once again it was a time for discussion and decision about their changing lives. Trang applied for maternity leave from the Gippsland Institute after completing the academic year there. Adding to their joy, David's parents offered to accommodate them during the remainder of Trang's pregnancy. Their home would be a good base for David's PhD studies as well, so the young couple took the decision to move to Melbourne. It was another turning point, changing their state orientation from New South Wales to Victoria while starting a family.

Trang recalls that an important factor in her acceptance of the invitation to move in with David's parents was that she had already formed a strong bond with Sadie. In contrast, Arthur had become even more reticent as he aged.

> He showed little interest, really. We lived in the same house, but all of my interaction and the strong support, all of my very close relationship really was with Sadie. David was the first son, and for years before his brother Christopher came along he was an only child. He had become extremely close to his mother. They would sit and chat until all hours, sometimes one or two o'clock in the morning. And, because of that, when I came along Sadie was so happy. I was the daughter that she never had.

> She was a professional dressmaker, and she said that for so many years she had to make only boys' clothes. It was so boring and after we became engaged she made me such beautiful clothes - coats, suits and even my going-away dress for our wedding. She was just so happy to make beautiful dresses for me. So we became very close, and she was one of the three or four women who have been most influential in my life. Her kindness to me always reminds me of how lucky I was to meet so many good women along the way, women who taught me so much

about the choices I had and how important it was to maintain purpose and faith in my abilities. Le was my first very close relationship, then there were the Salvation Army ladies, Miss Gale in particular. I learned such a lot; so many of my values came from her.

First daughter Elizabeth was born on 3 May 1974 with no complications. For Trang, the joy of motherhood left no doubt in her mind that family was and always would be her first priority. There would be room for work, too, of that she was certain. But first things first. She and David needed a place of their own.

Proud new mother Trang, with daughter Elizabeth, 1974.

- CHAPTER 18 -

First Child, First Home

Melbourne, 1974-75

Trang stayed home for a year after Elizabeth was born, enjoying the experience of being a mother and at that stage not greatly missing her role as lecturer. Too much else was happening. During that year she and David bought their first home, a modest house in Highbury Road, Glen Waverley. In the mid-1970s Glen Waverley was a much more rural area, a far cry from the expensive suburb of today. Cows grazed contentedly in a large paddock across from the house. There was little to remind them of the bustle of the city.

David was still in the first year of his PhD, with his scholarship bringing in a small amount that barely covered their living expenses. Trang thought often of her future, but without urgency. She was ready to be a mother and to stay home looking after Elizabeth, with part-time work an option to be explored when the time seemed right. Apart from her perennial anxiety about her family in Saigon, her major issue was one of loneliness.

It was her first taste of suburban isolation, the loss of regular social and work-related contact that afflicts so many stay-at-home mothers. During the long days she was alone with tiny Elizabeth, and she realised quite soon that she was fated to be an outsider in the neighbourhood. It seemed that the locals were already in cliques. The family next door was a typical Australian family, as were others further down the road. Their kids were mostly a little older than Elizabeth, one or two years old. The mothers went shopping and socialised together. No one around her showed any interest in the new Thomas family, signalling to her that neighbourhood groups were not easy to join. It probably did not help that she was clearly what was still called a

New Australian, an Asian one at that. Typically, she decided to try a positive approach instead of withdrawing further into her loneliness. She smiles as she recalls her move to break down the barriers to acceptance.

> I placed a notice in the local milk bar giving my details and saying that I would like to start a play group. My plan was that those mothers who joined, if any, would get together with their offspring to share experiences while the children played. To my surprise, several mothers responded to the notice.

> We met once a week, rotating from one house to another, having a cup of tea while the kids played together in the garden. And then we had a second round of kids, some went on to have their third and fourth. And we all stayed friends. We were all different, but we were just so supportive of each other because we were all lonely. Then, as time went on, new women would move into the locality. And somehow they would get the word about our group and contact us. At one stage our numbers grew to six or seven. It was then that we began to include our husbands. We started having dinners, and the men would get involved, even doing some of the cooking.

> There were people who left, too. But over the years a core group of five remained. We have stayed in touch over the forty years since, getting together several times a year and even travelling together when opportunity offered. In contrast, our children, who grew up as friends, got married and had their own families but did not maintain contact.

Trang still marvels that her initiative turned out so well. It is not at all surprising for those who know her for her problem-solving and people skills. Passive acceptance is not one of her qualities. Among her rewards is the gift of lasting friendships, valued people who stay in touch and catch up with her regularly.

Her problem of loneliness addressed, Trang soon decided that she needed more. The urge to work had returned. Elizabeth was a healthy and happy toddler, and David was engrossed in his studies. She read the job ads for local tertiary institutions and noted that the Royal Melbourne Institute of Technology (RMIT) was looking for a part-time psychology tutor. The job paid only $12 an hour, a pittance. Given her qualifications and experience, she was reluctant to show interest. David encouraged her to at least talk with the staff there in the hope that something better might come up.

Trang duly attended for an interview and agreed to give a few hours of her time weekly. It happened that RMIT had many part-time students who came in for their tutorials at night. That was more convenient for her, so she agreed to a part-time schedule of two to four hours per night. 'I think they were embarrassed about the $12 an hour.' She smiles at the memory. 'So they told me it was only the base rate. There would be extra money for marking and other tasks.'

Once more, Trang's willingness to meet her employer's needs in the short term stood her in good stead. She came to the notice of the head of department, who looked at her qualifications and areas of lecturing expertise. He was impressed. 'You have a master's degree with honours,' he said. 'You have lectured on the subject of Personality (Trang's specialty at the Gippsland Institute) and we are desperate for somebody to teach that particular topic. We have already advertised, but we could not find a suitable candidate.' She was surprised when the head offered her a job as full-time lecturer, but had to refuse.

'I am not ready for a full-time, permanent position,' she told him. 'I have a young child and my husband and I are planning another.'

The head persisted. 'We really need you. What would you say if we can organise your hours so that you don't have to come in every day. And a lot of your teaching would be at night anyway.'

Trang eventually agreed, the beginning of a long and fruitful association with RMIT. She recalls her pleasure at the unexpected outcome:

> It was not a job at the bottom of the ladder. They needed me more than I needed them, so they gave me a start at a higher level. And they were also very accommodating. They gave me two days when there was no teaching at all. So I didn't have to go in on those days. I could do my work at home. And there were another two days when I taught only at night. So I could look after Elizabeth, getting her ready for when David came home so that he could take over while I went to work. I would take the train to RMIT and give lectures to almost 200

students. It wasn't easy. After rising early and spending all day doing my thing with the house and baby, I was expected to perform intelligently for four hours at night. I did that for years, even after our second daughter, Helen, came along. But I was grateful to RMIT for allowing me a schedule that suited my needs. Staying at home for two full days was so helpful, and on the other three days Sadie would babysit. It was only Elizabeth at the start and I would take her down so she could look after her. None of my neighbours knew that I was working full time, as they frequently saw me at home during the days. So it was a very happy time, and I was a lecturer. For years I wasn't ambitious for more.

Trang's determined efforts to meet the joint challenges of motherhood and work during the mid-1970s are all the more remarkable given the many distractions arising from her family's circumstances. For it was just when she was getting back into the workforce that the war in Vietnam drew to its bitter close, bringing tragedy that exceeded her worst fears.

- CHAPTER 19 -

Saigon Falls

South Vietnam, April–May 1975

After the forces led by the United States left South Vietnam to fight on alone in 1972, North Vietnam had moved inexorably towards victory. Now the final offensive was under way and Trang's anxiety reached new heights. What if her family was trapped in Saigon? How could she help from so far away? Her status as an Australian citizen was of little help. Elizabeth was barely a toddler, so Trang could not go even if she were able to reach them. And with David studying there was little money to spare, even after she returned to work. Her mind churned with these thoughts even as she struggled with conflicting needs and priorities as a new mother just moving back into the workforce.

Saigon finally fell on 30 April 1975. Trang watched the news coverage grimly but little could be gleaned other than the news that the Americans were trying to evacuate those who had been placed at most risk through their former involvement with the Allied forces. Communication with her family was not possible, so she had no way of knowing that her parents and sister Chau were being evacuated as refugees to be resettled in the United States. She heard this news from Chau, who was in the final stage of pregnancy and struggling to keep the family group's move on track in the face of unexpected complications. As she wrote to Trang:

> We are having a terrible time. We are refugees again and this time it was hard because we were in such a hurry to leave along with everybody else. We tried to get out but we had no way and because my husband was in the military he could not get away without being regarded as a deserter. So he could not do anything about our situation. Then we had

some good news. There was a girl whose father was working for my brother and she worked for the American Embassy, only at a very low level but somehow she got a pass to go to America. Then her family decided they would not leave with her. She knew that we were in trouble so she offered to take us instead.

We were very lucky to get such an opportunity. So I gathered together our parents, my husband's parents and my three children. And I was eight months pregnant as well. I could barely walk and we got on the plane after two nights and our first stop was the Philippines. At that time Guam was the centre for refugees but the Americans had opened up another on Wake Island. So we were taken there, the first ones to arrive.

It seemed as if our escape was well under way but then our luck changed again. Mother suddenly became ill and the doctor said that she had septicaemia. She collapsed and was taken to the camp hospital. My husband said that for a time it seemed unlikely she would survive. But somehow she did recover. She said she had dreamed that she left us. She went back to the temple in Saigon, the temple where she used to go. And suddenly a friend of hers just took her hand. She called out, 'Where are you?' Then Mother woke up and an American nurse was tapping on her shoulder and she came back. And the nurse told my husband that we almost lost her. She was gone for a little while.

Her septicaemia was from a kidney infection. The Americans said they would take her and just my husband with her to Hawaii for an operation. They wanted my husband to be the interpreter during her treatment. But because I was about to have a child he said he could not leave his whole family to be with Mother. I went and saw the chief doctor and said: 'Please doctor, understand my situation. I have four elderly people, one sick. I have three young children and I am eight months pregnant. My husband is the only able-bodied person in the family and you are taking him away.' The doctor was very kind and he decided to let the whole family go to Hawaii. So Mother was taken to the hospital with my husband as interpreter and the rest of us are just leaving to follow them.

Trang was stunned by the news. She showed David the letter when he arrived home. 'I have to do something,' she said.

'That won't be easy,' said David. 'What do you want to do?'

'I want to bring them to Australia where we can help them. They are refugees. Surely there is a place here for them here if we agree to support them.'

'One would think so,' agreed David. 'But it might be very difficult. The word is that the prime minister is not interested in accepting refugees from Indochina.'

'I must try,' said Trang. 'I'll start by calling the Immigration Department to see what information and assistance I can request.'

The Immigration Department could not provide the answers Trang needed so she kept pushing, all the way up the line, finishing with a direct appeal to then Prime Minister Gough Whitlam. In response she eventually received a letter from a senior public servant saying there was nothing the Prime Minister could do. Trang was very angry, so angry that, although she had voted for Labor when Gough became PM, she now swore that she would never vote for his party again.

While Trang's disappointment was understandable, her appeals were very much against the odds. Australia was one of the first countries to recognise the new socialist government in Vietnam. Not surprisingly, the Whitlam Labor government wanted nothing to do with Indochinese refugee issues. The other factor was that the Americans had already accepted the family group and were doing their best for them. Trang later acknowledged that her family was probably better off going to the United States because the Americans had a much better system in place for looking after refugees. But, at the time, those considerations were overwhelmed by her frantic need to do something, anything, to help. Mother was very ill and nothing else mattered. So Trang tackled the issue head-on and refused to take no for an answer until all hope was exhausted.

Meanwhile, Chau kept them informed from Hawaii. By then Mother had undergone her operation to remove her diseased kidney, but afterwards her incision wound did not heal and she was being kept in a sterile room. It was four months before she was able to leave. Then came even worse news from Chau.

> I thought that father was okay. But he became very ill with diabetes. During all of that time of chaos when we fled from Saigon nobody had thought about giving him medication and he had not complained. So he was taken to the hospital for treatment, but when he was due for discharge he took a turn for the worse. He became delusional. They took him in for further treatment but he died yesterday. I am so sorry to have to tell you this news. Mother is still in the sterile room. I have told her and she is very sad.

That was on 23 May 1975. It was, of course, far too late for Trang to try to attend the funeral. While she had never been close to her father, her duty to him was clear. More importantly, Mother would miss him badly and would need support if and when she recovered. Trang felt deeply frustrated, so anxious and yet so helpless. The one piece of good news in that time was that Chau had her baby, her last child, on 12 June. It was a boy, the first American citizen in the family. She called him Andrew.

Mother eventually recovered from her post-surgery complications and, in her strong and pragmatic way, came to grips with the loss of her husband. The refugee group was moved onto the United States mainland to commence resettlement procedures. Trang and David provided whatever financial support they could, even borrowing money for the purpose. There was little else to be done, and in any case the fallout from the war had not by any means run its course. Most of Trang's siblings and their families were still trapped in Saigon. It was soon after that the tragic news came from Kim.

- CHAPTER 20 -

Tragedy at Sea

Saigon, late 1975

Kim and her family were in all sorts of trouble. Her account of the time following North Vietnam's victory is matter of fact but poignant.

> All of us tried to get away, but we failed. When Saigon fell, Chau's family had to go right away because they were in great danger. The young lady who helped my parents and her family to leave Vietnam left with them. So I didn't know anybody who could help. It was too late for us. We tried many times to escape by boat, but we did not have enough money for people to help us to get away. So we failed.
>
> Before Saigon fell, we were reasonably rich. I had shares in three big pharmaceutical and insurance companies. I had been successful in my career as a pharmacist and I was the CEO of another pharmaceutical company. When it became obvious in 1975 that the war was lost, I pulled out some of my money from investment companies and invested in gold and jewellery. After the war I lost everything I had in the bank and my remaining business investments so I had less and less for our needs. Everything now belonged to the state. And even the money we had was almost worthless - 500 piastres to buy one American dollar. So we lost everything, really. Even my jewellery, diamonds and gold, which we sold to try to escape. We tried to sell the furniture, the television, the refrigerator. Everything. We had to sell to eat, and because we were trying to escape we didn't want to keep those things. We needed to go, not stay. But the terrible thing that happened was not losing money, but losing three of our children. It was no longer about money. Money you can gain back but not your kids.

> It happened because, when we trying to escape, there was not enough money for all of us to go together. We had five children. So my middle three kids went with their nanny, while my eldest and youngest stayed behind with us. The next month my oldest son went by boat and he was successful. He was rescued by an American ship. We do not know what happened to our other three children and the nanny. They were never seen again. So my husband and I, and the youngest girl, stayed in Saigon. Because by then we had nothing left to try again.

Trang thought desperately of ways and means to help Kim and her family to flee the communist regime. The only good news was that they continued to survive. Fortunately, neither Kim nor her husband were persecuted beyond the forfeiture of their possessions because they had not been involved in any way with the former government. Kim's husband was a teacher who had taught in private schools on a typically low salary. And, while Kim had been a very successful businesswoman, she also had no links to officialdom. For that reason they were allowed to stay and eke out a living as best they could. Trang was eventually able to get money to Kim on a regular basis to help. But nothing could help Kim or her husband come to grips with the loss of their three children. Trang, too, shed many tears for them, and David, distraught and feeling helpless, could only be supportive while his wife's grief ran its course.

As if Kim's tragic losses, the death of their father, Mother's long illness and the ongoing drama of Chau's family group moving to the United States were not traumatic enough, more bad news followed. Trang's brother Quynh, who was sixteen when the family fled from North Vietnam in 1954, had gone on to study medicine and duly graduated as a doctor. He was later forced to join the South Vietnamese Army, where he also trained as a paratrooper so that he could be dropped into battle zones to treat the wounded. He was looked upon as a hero by the family. After Saigon fell, he was detained and sent to a re-education camp. He never returned, and was last seen by his sister Dung when she was allowed to visit him at the camp. No one was sure, but it later appeared that he had died in 1977.

The news of Quynh's departure for the brainwashing camp weighed heavily on Trang as she counted the growing toll on her family taken by the war. It had literally been torn apart. Now that she was working as a lecturer again, she and David could provide a measure of financial support to the survivors. Though generous, what they could afford seemed pitifully inadequate. And there was still more to come. Kim was not the only one trapped in Saigon. Dung, Phuong and Dzi were still fighting their own battles there. It was more than three years before they too escaped as boat people, opening the way to an unlikely adventure for Trang and David. In the meantime, there was more than enough to occupy them in their own lives.

- CHAPTER 21 -

Consolidation and Crisis

Melbourne, 1977-79

For Trang and David, the family tragedies ensuing from the fall of Saigon were followed by a period of consolidation - continuing study for David and Trang's ever-busy life as lecturer by night and housewife and mother by day. There were two very notable events in 1977. The first of these was the arrival of second daughter Helen on 25 September.

Elizabeth was growing quickly, a bright and engaging child who would soon be ready for kindergarten. 'The first thing I remember is Helen coming home,' she says. 'I was almost four. We went to visit her in hospital because she was premature.'

Trang and Helen did well following the premature birth and the family adapted quickly to the needs of its new member. Their first home seemed to be shrinking as their number grew, so it was time to move. They found a more suitable family home a short distance away in Orchard Street, Glen Waverley and quickly settled back into their routine. David, having completed the first two years of his PhD, was now engaged in two years of part-time study with the aim of finishing his thesis in 1978. Trang continued her lecturing duties at RMIT, a more difficult fit now with a second child. It was a time for counting blessings. They had so much for to look forward to and they had their two precious girls. However, despite the happiness of family and academic progress, the late 1970s became an ever more demanding period because of the need to balance so many competing requirements.

The support they were providing to family members in Saigon and the United States was a heavy drain on their finances, a testament to both Trang's dedication to her kinship responsibilities and David's generous support. One source of anxiety was at least partially removed when Chau's group was resettled in Minnesota. They had been sponsored by the Lutheran Church and were very well treated when they arrived. Chau's husband found work straight away as a production-line worker, a position well below his capabilities as a former senior officer but he was grateful for the opportunity. Chau too found employment some time later as a filing clerk. She eventually rose to a supervisory position as a bookkeeper and concurrently studied to requalify as a pharmacist in the United States. But initially it was a difficult time on low wages, and Trang continued to subsidise their income. She felt an overwhelming need to see her refugee family, especially Mother. She saved carefully for fares and, in June 1978, as soon as Helen was old enough to undertake the journey, she visited Mother and Chau in Minnesota and Le in Canada. It was an exhausting effort with her two young daughters, Helen still in her first year. Both were ill on the long flight to Los Angeles. Despite her weariness, Trang was overjoyed to be reunited with her family for the first time since visiting Saigon with David shortly after their marriage. It had been eight long years.

It was also her first opportunity to show Mother her latest grandchildren. Now elderly, Mother was finding it difficult to cope. Widowed and isolated from all that she had known, she had also left her three sons behind in Saigon. By then, Dzi had followed Quynh to the re-education camps because he too had served in the South's army. Luckily, he was allowed to rejoin his family following a period of indoctrination. Phuong was much older, so he escaped the re-education process. Even so, he and his family had been badly affected by the harshness of the changes that the new government had introduced. In all of the brothers' minds the need to escape was uppermost and, although they were never to see Quynh again, the others would continue to work towards joining the ranks of the boat people.

When Trang returned from her family reunion, it was still in her mind that she'd be content with her master's degree and the ongoing balancing act of staying home with the children as much as possible while keeping her much-needed position at RMIT. After all, she reasoned, there were many who spent their careers and retired as lecturers. It was a comfortable job at a reasonable salary level, not lucrative but not at the bottom either. Then there was David. Trang told herself that he had his career to build and that her supporting role and work as a lecturer should be enough for her.

Unfortunately, an issue arose that would eventually precipitate a crisis in the marital relationship. It began in 1978, when David was still working towards his PhD at Monash. He was greatly enjoying the experience, mixing with some very stimulating people at the various functions he attended there. Some of the professors would host dinner parties, inviting the postgraduate students to come along with their spouses. Trang would attend these functions with David. She looked forward to the occasions at first but, to her dismay, these very interesting people who were her husband's friends treated her as an inferior. They would discuss all sorts of topics and if she tried to join in they would quickly dismiss her views. She recalls one particular evening when some very young Monash lecturers were discussing student issues, matters that she was very familiar with because she, too, was a lecturer with substantial experience.

> I joined in the discussion about techniques of teaching and they just dismissed me. Like, you are only the wife of a postgraduate student. How dare you join in this lofty conversation? So I was very upset at that kind of experience. They were so young and said such hurtful things. There was another night when they wanted to go off and drive for an hour to get a special pizza. The best pizza in Melbourne, they said. And so they all got into the car to go and David was so excited about joining them but I said, 'We have two kids. We are not going to put them into a car and drive for an hour just to get a pizza. If these young people want to search for a gourmet pizza they can but we are at a different stage of life. I would rather go home and settle the kids.'

> So we had a lot of disagreements in this way. All sorts of different issues. We were moving further apart while he was mixing with these young academics. And there I was with two little kids and if I tried to join in they would dismiss me. So for that reason I decided that I could not stay as a wife and mother forever. It became clear to me that I really needed to have my own career, my own identity. That's when I said that perhaps I should go back and do my PhD so that I would be less dependent. The issues continued and we nearly decided to divorce at one stage. Luckily for me, Sadie was very supportive. When she realised

the extent of our problems she said, 'Bring the kids home to me and I'll deal with David. You will be with me and we will support you.'

Fortunately, that situation did not arise. However, Trang was not alone in deciding that she should study for her doctorate. One of her mentors, a senior lecturer at RMIT who was one of the first women at the top in psychology, returned to Australia with a PhD from the University of London. In those days that was a really big deal. She encouraged Trang to go through with her plan because she needed to move on from being a lecturer with very little scope for real progress. But still Trang hesitated. It was a big decision to go back to study because so much time had passed since her postgraduate studies at Macquarie and so much had changed, including the technology. The day of the computer had arrived.

'I didn't even know what a computer looked like,' she says. 'So I was really very reluctant because I had missed so much. But I was still being urged to do my PhD and that reinforced my urge to go further.'

These relationship and career issues were very much on Trang's mind in early 1979 when news came that her oldest sister Dung and brothers Phuong and Dzi, together with their families, had escaped by boat from Saigon. Once more, love of family came to the fore.

Second daughter Helen's christening, Melbourne, 1977.

CHAPTER 21 - Consolidation and Crisis

David graduates from Monash University with PhD in Economics, 1978.

- CHAPTER 22 -

Escape from Saigon

MV *Marguerite*, Mekong River, February 2014

Trang was glad to relax into the comfort of the upper-deck stateroom. She and David had long looked forward to their cruise down the Mekong, one of the great rivers of Asia. They had spent several days in the Cambodian tourist hotspot of Siem Reap, enjoying the tuk-tuk rides and visits to the fabled temples of the region. Now it was time to explore the wide brown river, pausing to shop at riverside villages and the Cambodian capital of Phnom Penh. The tour would finish in Ho Chi Minh City, always in her memory as Saigon.

There was much on her mind, but she never tired of her travels. And this trip was special because David was accompanying her. She also had the company of two of her sisters, Kim and Chau, her cousin Kim Chi and her best friend, Lorraine Elliott. Then there were colleagues and friends, among the latter the war veteran she had laughingly appointed her historian two years earlier in Hanoi. He had since begun to write her biography.

'You and Robyn must join us on this cruise,' Trang had urged. 'This will be your chance to record interviews with my family members and my friend Lorraine. She knows so much about me. And you will be great company for David. He has a story to tell you about the time when three of my siblings and their families were boatpeople. It is too good a chance to miss.'

Pulau Bidong Refugee Centre: Malaysia, January–March 1979

Trang had been delighted to hear that Dung, Phuong and Dzi, together with their children, had escaped by boat to Malaysia's Pulau Bidong (Bidong

Island) refugee centre. Dzi had managed to get letters out to say that the group was safe and awaiting processing as refugees.

'We must go there,' she said to David. They discussed the possibilities and agreed to go, hoping to somehow find a way to visit the refugee centre. David's succinct account of the following weeks speaks clearly of both his initiative and his ability to play a role convincingly:

> We had a few Malaysian friends but they were unable to exercise any influence to get us onto the island. The authorities didn't want to know us. The tricky bit was that the island was several miles offshore and entry was restricted to those whose contribution to the refugees' welfare had been approved. There was a security point that nobody was allowed to pass unless they had the right permit. And to get a permit involved not only credible cover but also a lot of red tape. So we travelled to Merang in Terengganu Province, the nearest point on the mainland to Pulau Bidong, to see what we could do. The town had one hotel where most of the public servants doing screening tests for migrants stayed, especially the British, Americans and Australians.

> So far so good, and we came up with a plan. Not a good plan, but nothing else came to mind. Trang stayed in our room while I mixed a great deal with these officials to get to be known. I managed to enlist the aid of a group of Americans, who kindly helped me to go with them on a boat trip to the island. At that point I had large numbers of American dollars stuffed down my underpants and a big suitcase and I bluffed my way into the camp. Fortunately, because I was with the American group and they had the necessary permits, the guard patrol just seemed to think that I should be there and when they queried me I was very caustic and short with them. 'Of course I'm bloody-well supposed to be here.' So they just let me pass.

> Somehow I got that bit right, so I kept on and asked to see Trang's youngest brother, Dr Dzi. He was one of those who had not been all that keen on our marriage. I remember to this day the look on his face when he came into the interview room. I was an important person, of course, if I was going to interview him. I said, 'Dr Dzi?' and he very

warily said, 'Yeeess?' So I said, 'I'm David Thomas. I married your sister Trang.'

The relief on his face was profound. I asked him if I could see the rest of his group so he brought around the other members of the family. We all huddled into this interview room and I just gave them the food in the suitcase I had brought and the American dollars. The island had this amazing little economy going. If you had American dollars, you could secure yourself a little plot of land and set up your campsite in a really good space close to the cooking tents and the water supply. If you didn't, you were out in the backblocks somewhere under the palm trees and making do as best you could. And they had no idea, of course, how long they were going to be there, so it was essential that they get set up properly. They needed mostly one-dollar notes so they could buy fish and vegetables from the locals, who brought fresh food from the mainland by boat. Surprisingly, Trang and I were lucky to be able to arrange large numbers of single dollars through a local bank.

So that was day one of my deception. As we were leaving, I made a point of talking to the guards who patrolled the camp. I was pleasant and chummy, sharing cigarettes and generally establishing goodwill. After that I was Dr Thomas and I could return the next day. Before long I began to take Trang as my nurse assistant. The story was that we were there to investigate certain health problems. The guys on the gate saw me regularly, part of the same group, and accepted that she was my assistant. That was the tricky bit, bluffing our way into the camp. I was getting good at it by then and once we were in there it didn't matter. We could move around freely.

While we were there, one of the refugee boats turned up with a Malaysian Navy escort vessel. The Malaysian sailors came onshore. Among them was a quite senior navy officer, and for some reason he took a shine to me and we had long conversations about the problems of the world and the refugee boats. Stuff like that. I walked around the camp with him for a while and made it obvious that he and I were best mates.

> So my efforts to infiltrate the camp kept working and I never had any problems with any of the officials. The nearest I got to getting into strife was with this Swedish journalist who, when we were about to get onto one of the boats to go to the island one day, insisted on pulling out his pass card and showing it to the guards. I thought, if they ask me for a pass card, I don't have one. So I wandered off and thought about my chances of pushing him over the side but I resisted the impulse. He was a very naive guy for a journalist. Anyway, we were still getting away with it, passing ourselves off as a doctor and nurse, and we were able to give Trang's relatives a fair bit of money and support before we left to come back to Australia. They were eventually accepted for resettlement in the United States.

Trang recalls her joy and relief at the success of their mission:

> I was not only greatly relieved that we could help, but also because David's efforts on Pulau Bidong finally put paid to residual concerns by some in my family that I had made an inappropriate marriage. I was always praised for my generosity in helping all of my family members after Saigon fell, but I insisted that full credit must also go to David, who willingly gave as my partner. Without him it would not have been possible to give as freely and that would have meant even more hardship.
>
> I have always believed that the more you give, the more you will receive. That was what Mother instilled in all of us, always leading the way by example. And by 'the more you will receive' I don't mean that I expect to be repaid. I mean that it's my family and there's nothing more important than that and to see my surviving relatives happy now is beyond any thought of price.
>
> Our shared mission to Pulau Bidong also did much to restore our relationship. A major difficulty had been that David was prone to depressive episodes, a curse he suffered throughout his life. He received treatment when necessary, but to me it often seemed that I was somehow failing him in my efforts to improve his mood. I too sought counselling, eventually accepting advice that it was not my

responsibility to ensure that David was happy all of the time. That was a big leap for me. It meant that I didn't get so upset or guilty when he was struggling to stay on an even keel.

So it transpired that the Pulau Bidong episode was a key turning point, not least because Trang could now put aside the most pressing of the family concerns that had plagued her for so long. There was still much of the academic road ahead and the next step was higher qualifications. David had just completed his PhD and would be returning to the workforce. That meant less of a struggle to make ends meet while she studied. It was time, she decided, to get on with it.

- CHAPTER 23 -

Trang's Thesis

Melbourne 1979-88

Despite her renewed enthusiasm, Trang did not rush into her PhD studies. Her first priority was to consolidate the progress she and David had made despite the difficulties and crises of the past several years. With her lecturer position at RMIT well established and Elizabeth beginning her school years, Melbourne remained their preferred place of residence, although, for David, staying there offered limited employment options. At that time, Monash had a policy of not employing its own graduates, whereas Melbourne University preferred to do the opposite. So two major universities were virtually closed shops to David.

In 1979, he worked for nine months as a lecturer at Caulfield Technical College before finding a position as senior lecturer at Swinburne University. A year later, he became acting head of the Economics Department when the incumbent took leave of absence. The incumbent did not return, so David was confirmed in the position. It had been a rapid rise through the ranks for him, and was a welcome advance to greater financial security. The years had been lean since the children were born, even after Trang found her position at RMIT. There had been the costs of housing and continuing assistance to Trang's family. Now it was time to plan for their daughters' education. He and Trang were determined to give them a good start in life.

While Trang was still considering research topics for her own doctorate, David was enjoying his position and a growing reputation as a productive researcher. As well, his job provided him with a measure of flexibility that was welcome in terms of his being able to play a stronger role supporting Trang in her work–life balance and thus facilitate her intended return to study. David also appreciated the flexibility offered by his position:

> The nicest thing about academic life is that the job has to get done but you can pretty much choose your own working time. You can work all weekend and take days off during the week. And of course you can work all weekend and not take days off. It's pretty much up to you. I found that research came fairly easily to me so I could produce a couple of articles a year without too much stress. And that was enough to keep me in good standing as an academic.

By 1981, Trang had thought long and hard about a suitable area for her own research. She was strongly inclined towards the psychological issues of ageing. But with typical thoroughness, she didn't rush her decision. She really wanted to make sure that ageing was her first choice as a field of study, so she first laid the foundation with a six-month sabbatical in geriatrics. The Mount Royal National Research Institute for Gerontology and Geriatric Medicine, located at Melbourne's Mount Royal Hospital, was her obvious choice. The director, Professor Derek Prinsley, had been appointed by Melbourne University as foundation chair in geriatrics and gerontology in 1976. In this position, he was the leader in a field which had previously attracted comparatively little interest. Trang explains:

> Who wanted to study old people? The feeling was that they were dying anyway. You treat them and they die. They never get better. Whereas with children, if you cure them there's a whole life ahead. That is a much more satisfactory outcome. So nobody in medicine wanted to do ageing. In psychology it was even worse. It really didn't exist.

It was at Mount Royal that Trang met sociologist Anna Howe, the first person in Australia doing serious research into ageing. They discussed the possibilities and she encouraged Trang to find a supervisor who would be willing to supervise a thesis in that field. Trang had heard at La Trobe University of Professor Ray Over's reputation as a supervisor. She arranged a meeting to tell him of her interest in research into ageing and to sound him out as a potential supervisor. He looked keenly at her and asked why she wanted to study old people. He said he could suggest other topics that would be much more exciting. For example, he was looking for someone to study the differences between boys and girls in the study of mathematics. That would be a much more interesting topic and so much easier for Trang to carry out a project. She could just go to a school and talk to the principal and he would provide the children for the study. But to make a study of old people she would have to go into nursing homes and that would be so depressing. Trang was amused, but not convinced:

> He tried to talk me out of it! But I persisted with the approach that I really wanted to do something on older people. I felt that everybody seemed to be concentrating on studies of children and young adults and if I completed my PhD on younger people I would be just one of many. But, if my studies were on adjustment to ageing, I would be different. I would be one of the leaders in that field. There would be little competition. Professor Over agreed to be my supervisor and years later, when I had completed my research, he was very happy about it. We still keep in touch.

There was also an unexpected development that bolstered Trang's confidence. When she talked with Professor Over and showed him her record he was very impressed by her first-class honours. In academia, firsts are special. Recipients are rated among the top one per cent of students. So he recommended that the dean award Trang a full-time scholarship. She couldn't believe her good fortune. She would be able to conduct her research and studies full time for two and a half years before returning to her lecturer post at RMIT to finish her thesis part time.

Trang looked forward to commencing her studies. She had put a great deal of thought, and the knowledge gained from her sabbatical, into working out exactly where she wanted to go with her research and the method she would use. She decided on a longitudinal study of the effects on the wellbeing of older people of having to move into residential care. There were three phases in her research. First, she recruited subjects, meeting them for an initial interview shortly before they moved into a nursing home or hostel. This was a key time to record their emotional states and concerns while they were in the process of packing up their homes or lying in hospital waiting for a placement. To find her subjects, she enlisted the aid of accommodation officers in various helping organisations and hospitals.

These helpers would assist by notifying Trang of patients and clients due for placement within three or four weeks and facilitating contact to discuss their participation in the study. If they agreed, Trang would visit them to talk in the pre-admission phase and then again approximately three months after their move. The second visit was all about how well they had settled in. She followed up with a third visit a year after their admission. So in a total of three interviews she looked very carefully at how each participant coped with their changed circumstances.

Trang's thesis also assessed the quality of residential facilities and the impact of that aspect on patient wellbeing. As she proceeded with her examination of a broad cross-section of facilities and the wellbeing of their clients, she became more and more convinced that the psychological aspect of moving into care was so much more important to residents than money or the quality of their new homes. She explains:

> I learned so much. For example, at the top level the standard of accommodation and services was comparable to five star hotels and was similarly expensive. The clients had their own rooms with ensuite plus sit-down meals with choice of courses and wine. At the other end of the scale were low-quality homes more like old-style rooming houses, especially those for men only. In these very basic facilities, I would find two or three men sharing a room with poor furnishings and smelly, dirty carpets. In response to my queries, the owners would tell me that these were the men who had nowhere else to go. Many were alcoholics. Putting in new carpets was a waste of time and money because they would quickly be covered with cigarette burns. 'There's just no point in doing it unless residents have some respect for their environment,' was their bottom line.

In between these extremes there was of course a broad spectrum of facilities. Trang developed a measure to rate homes from very good to very poor in various aspects of quality. And while one might logically expect to find a clear link between quality and client wellbeing, her findings were that quality played an unexpectedly small part:

> Residents in top quality homes could still be very unhappy. Conversely, among those in very low-quality homes I found many residents who

were grateful just to have a roof over their heads. They were the ones who had absolutely no one else to care for them. Many had relatives, including children, who did not want to visit them because of their background or for whatever reason. So they tended to be grateful for any assistance and relatively contented. In quality homes, however, wellbeing was affected by more complex issues. For example, these residents were often parents of children who had become very, very successful in business, but they themselves could be from very humble beginnings. And now that their successful children had put them into the best homes money could buy, they just didn't fit in. I remember there was a lady in tears who said to me that all of the other ladies in the home would laugh at her because she didn't know as much as they did. Like the time there was a dish on the menu called Chicken Fricassee and she didn't know what it meant. She asked the lady alongside her and the lady just laughed at her. She felt so humiliated, so unhappy. And she was in the most expensive home in Melbourne. And I also found that a most important factor in moving to a nursing home is coping. Coping and solving problems. Because I remember another lady who was very unhappy. She complained because her neighbour in the next room did this and did that. And I suggested to her that she might quietly ask the manager to move her to another room. Every problem has a solution. But she just kept saying 'No! No! No!' So that's a case of someone not bothering to cope, not bothering to attempt problem-solving. And when I came to see her after twelve months, I found that she had died already. I was not surprised, simply because she had not tried to improve her situation and so she just remained very unhappy.

Trang thus found that attitude was a key determinant of adjustment and wellbeing in the aged. In almost all circumstances in which a resident entered care, there was good and bad in the situation in which they found themselves. It was a resident's attitude to adjustment that counted, how they tried to cope or to deal with the situation. The time before moving in was especially important: the mental preparation for and acceptance of change. Family support counted a great deal. Trang recalls one very well-known person who was particularly unhappy. When she talked to him she found that his cognitive functioning was apparently unimpaired. There was a pile of scientific journals in his room that he still read. He showed her the medals and awards he had won for high achievement. But he was just so unhappy that he could not adjust to his new circumstances. His life had become very difficult when his health deteriorated. His wife had been unable to cope, so she had to put him into the home. It was very nice, of course. He had a beautiful room of his own. But, when Trang was with him, he just cried, a man who was mentally sound but physically ill. He just wanted to go home.

Not surprisingly, Trang's research also led her to conclude that the social side of ageing, the support of family, friends and networks, was very important in achieving acceptance and contentment. Her interviews also showed clearly that satisfaction with life achievements was a vital part of contentment in old age. Her finding was that people should be encouraged to pursue during their retirement the goals they had to defer or forego during their working lives, no matter how modest or challenging. She explains that this was a key factor:

> When the time comes for them to be dependent on aged care, if they have regrets they are more likely to be about what they didn't get to do than the things they've done that turned out to be mistakes. Regret is a most destructive emotion. So the moral of the story is that, if you have an urge to try something new, go for it. Better not to die thinking 'What if?'

By 1983, Trang's research was under way and the necessary adjustments to household routines were settling into place. With their relationship back on track, positive goals set and the bonus of continuing childcare support from David's mother, she and David were able to focus on their academic pursuits. At long last their lives were more predictable and they could concentrate on their daughters' educational and social development.

- CHAPTER 24 -

New Times, New Goals

Melbourne, 1983-88

Commencing her PhD studies was, for Trang, yet another pivotal point. She was full of ideas, her own ideas, and now it was time for her to put them out there for comment. She had also taken another positive step by becoming more involved with her professional body, the Australian Psychological Society (APS), as the Victorian State Coordinator of the newly formed APS Women and Psychology Interest Group. This somewhat controversial addition to the range of APS members' activities arose from a women's meeting at an annual APS Conference. Their aim was to establish a group that would be granted formal status in the APS to examine research into women's issues in the profession and how their counterparts in the American Psychological Association approached those issues. The meeting was instigated by a NSW psychologist and strongly supported by Trang's former supervisor and mentor, Dr Una Gault. Dr Gault was of course a well-known feminist and determined advocate for women's voices to be heard. Trang recalls the reaction to the initiative with amusement:

> We held the meeting, and it was interrupted by our male colleagues, who just didn't think it was right. It was their view that issues in psychology were neither men's nor women's issues, but were common to all psychologists. My previous supervisor at Macquarie, John Collins, who was also an ex-president of the APS, was particularly incensed by the idea that women should have their own special issues to address. In the face of such trenchant disapproval, the ladies didn't succeed in establishing the national group that they'd envisaged, but did manage to establish interest groups in their individual states. I became the Victorian Coordinator.

> I made a lot of good friends through that position, and I got to know some more feminists. I set up a meeting each month in a restaurant, and would find guest speakers to address the gathering. Typically they would be women, but once I invited a male to come along. It was my PhD supervisor and I thought he would present an interesting topic. But some of the women said, 'No! We don't want males coming along to lecture us.' Yet it was a good group, very supportive. Some of the members were professors, skilled in various areas of research. I learned a lot from them. These days it is a recognised interest group within the APS, counting for professional development points like other activities. It is even more a feminist group now, not concerned with specific issues of women in psychology. So people don't join if they are not particularly engaged in the broader feminist movement. I still go along occasionally, when I have time. They tend to be younger people now. Their goals are to encourage research into women's issues and to award prizes to those who do significant research. They run workshops along those lines. Sometimes they have different initiatives, depending upon who is running the group that year. I also belong to an interest group concerned with the issues of ageing.

Having arranged her professional engagement to her satisfaction, Trang could concentrate on her doctoral research. David later described the interval between 1983 and 1989 as the years when they were just plugging along, getting established as academics and moving up the scale.

> In my case that happened quite quickly. And then it was just doing the job. We actually worked in pretty well together. Trang had supported me enormously while I was doing my PhD, and when our roles were reversed I supported her while she was studying. I was pretty good at the basic cleaning and fixing up, looking after the kids, that kind of thing. Couldn't cook for nuts, of course. I eventually did take up cooking, but that came much later. And there was another plus. We were both extremely busy at the time, but on the other hand we were both in the same profession. When one of us had to go to a conference, it was often possible for the other to arrange something so that we could go together. That was important, because it meant that we didn't

have to be separated as much as we might have been.'

First daughter Elizabeth provided interesting insight into her parents' attention to childhood learning as she and Helen grew up in a household where study was the norm:

> We kids saw both our mother and father writing papers and marking papers all the time. And there was constant participation in our own studies and help with our homework. Reading with us, doing all sorts of activities with us so it was always a very supportive learning environment. That's the sort of thing that we are now trying to replicate with our kids as well. Our kids are interested in reading and writing and we play maths games with them and that's the other thing my parents were doing, making learning fun by building it into our everyday activities. So we had reading games, literacy games and numeracy games. I think it was a long time before I realised that our parents were using Monopoly to teach us maths. It was never good enough just to roll the dice. We had to add them up first, and then count the spaces. It was like that with other everyday things, like going to the shops. Working out how much each item added to the overall cost. And they made sure that all learning was relevant to our lives. That's what I do now with my girls when we take them to the shops. We talk about, like, if I've got five dollars and what I want costs three dollars, then how much do I have left? It's just everyday learning.
>
> Our parents valued having a well-rounded experience. They took Helen and me out of school for a trip to Europe and America. So I think that it wasn't just a focus on academic study for them, but also on a wider sense of world experience. And getting a feel for history. The year that we travelled to Europe was the year I was studying its history. So it was amazing going to all those places, like seeing where the Wars of the Roses happened and visiting Versailles, where Marie Antoinette lived. Just at the time when I was learning about those periods.

Trang too recalls the girls' reactions to the many wonders they saw, including the expression on Helen's face as she stood looking at the Pyramids of Giza.

'Whose idea was it to bring us here?' she asked. She just couldn't believe she was there, enjoying that wonderful experience. So we aimed in those ways to expand their learning experiences beyond schoolwork. At times we overdid it, like when we took them to Westminster Abbey. 'Why do we have to stand around here learning about all of these dead people?' asked Helen.

The mid-1980s also saw the family move from Glen Waverley to Kew, first to Mount Street in 1984, when Elizabeth and Helen moved from Wesley College to enrol as students at the Methodist Ladies College (MLC), and then to 28 Lofts Avenue in 1986. The latter address had the advantage of being opposite the girls' new school, where they would complete their secondary education before going on to Melbourne University.

The change of school for the girls arose from Trang's disappointment with the attitude of Elizabeth's classroom teacher at Wesley. Elizabeth and Helen had commenced their studies there not long after the college, formerly a boys' school, began to take girls. Only about 30 per cent of students in the primary school were female. Trang recalls that Helen was quite strong but Elizabeth was very shy. So she was bullied. Her class was full of unkind boys. At a parent–teacher interview, her teacher told Trang that Elizabeth was such a good girl. She would always sit in the corner doing her work. 'Most of the time,' said the teacher, 'I hardly even know that she is there.' Trang was not impressed. She and David were battling to pay the school fees and she wasn't about to part with so much money to have Elizabeth sit in a corner unnoticed.

Their decision to move the girls to the MLC led to a sound outcome. Elizabeth and Helen were happy at the MLC. Both she and Elizabeth made good friends at the college, friendships they still maintain. The fees became more affordable when Helen won a scholarship to take her through the secondary level. Along the way both girls excelled at extracurricular activities. Elizabeth was an extremely good swimmer and became school captain for that sport. They both took singing lessons, and here it was Helen who excelled. She went on to sing in Melbourne opera productions and stage musicals.

By the time the girls were well settled in at the MLC, Trang had completed her full-time scholarship at La Trobe University and had returned to her lecturer position at RMIT. There she faced the task of completing her thesis while working full time. She recalls that it was a demanding period:

> It was hard, writing it up after I went back to RMIT. Like the proverbial sword hanging over one's head. I used to tell my students that I would get up at four in the morning, and I would write until five or six before I went back to bed. The kids would wake at seven and I'd be up again to get them to school and then go to work. From that aspect I did the final years of my PhD the hard way, the same way that David had completed his thesis. We were very poor when he began to study for his doctorate, living on his scholarship with two little kids. I really had to go back to work when Elizabeth was still a toddler because we were sending money to my family as well. They were hard years. So I told my students I knew about hardship and poverty. There was no point in their complaining about it to me.

In 1987 Trang delivered her first research paper overseas at a psychology conference in Montreal, Canada. Then, in 1988, she was promoted to senior lecturer at RMIT. It was another important step up the ladder but her expectations remained modest. Her PhD would qualify her to contest higher academic positions, to perhaps be offered opportunities that would not otherwise be offered. So, as she pushed herself hard to complete her thesis, her major asset was her faith in her ability to follow whatever path opened for her as Dr Trang. Fittingly, she dedicated her work to her children: 'To Elizabeth and Helen, my two daughters, to whom the joy of my old age I entrust.' She smiles broadly when she recalls their typically Australian response. 'We will find you a very good nursing home,' they laughed when they saw it. That time has not yet come, but if it does, Trang will be comforted by her compliance with her own research findings. She will not spend her days regretting lost opportunities or thinking about adventures she might have had if there had just been time.

- CHAPTER 25 -

Doctor Trang

Melbourne, 1989-91

Trang was awarded her PhD in 1989, seven years after commencing her studies at La Trobe University and following closely her promotion to senior lecturer at RMIT the previous year. Both achievements fulfilled her aim of making the 1980s a decade of solid progress in her academic career. It was very satisfying too that David had enjoyed notable success since graduating with his PhD in 1979. Both had come a long way since leaving Sydney in 1972 to take up positions at the Riverina CAE. One might have expected that, moving into the 1990s, they would be content to continue their successful careers and enjoy the fruits of their hard work.

Those who knew Trang and David well would not have shared this view. They were both too engaged with the world around them to rest on their laurels. The early 1990s would see David take leave of absence from Swinburne University to undertake a key advisory role in Victorian Liberal politics, that of chief economic adviser to opposition leaders Alan Brown and his successor, Jeff Kennett. The policies of Cain and Kirner Labor governments had sparked social and economic controversy, resulting in a concerted push by the conservative opposition to regain power. David was keen to play his part in the campaign for economic reform.

Meanwhile, Trang's PhD led quickly to advancement. A number of factors came together to open up new opportunities, the first her own foresight in selecting the field of ageing for her PhD thesis. The second was that RMIT was transitioning to full university status, an expansion that required the establishment of foundation chairs in all faculties. As well, a Centre for Applied Social Research was set up to provide facilities for its staff and students comparable to that of existing universities. Enter Trang, already building a formidable reputation as a researcher and, despite her position towards the bottom of the senior lecturer rankings, well qualified for promotion. In 1990, she was appointed as director of the new centre. She quickly proved her worth to the RMIT establishment by bringing in large amounts of grant money, an essential virtue for one with leadership responsibilities in research. And that success was largely attributable to her new status as a leading expert in the field of ageing, an emerging economic and social issue that was now attracting serious attention from both sides of politics.

An important follow-up to her original research was the publication of *New Land, Last Home* in 1993, a study undertaken with fellow researcher Mark Balnaves for the Bureau of Immigration and Population Research. The study dealt with the experiences and reactions of older Vietnamese immigrants who came to Australia under the Family Migration Program. Trang explains:

> It is a much different experience from those who migrate young, work and then grow old. Those who migrate when they are old not only have to cope with all of the changes inherent in moving to a new country and culture, including the language barrier, but also the changes involved in growing old: declining health and the loss of mobility and independence.

This study was but one element of an impressive body of research that would be driven by Trang at RMIT. During this period, the fiscal implications of support for an ageing population became an important element of government consideration and planning. The major issue was the affordability of not only the age pension, but also care for the frail aged in light of rapidly increasing longevity and the anticipated impact of large numbers of retirements over a relatively short period when the postwar 'baby boomers' reached the end of their working lives. The Hawke government decided it was time to act, announcing a superannuation guarantee scheme to be funded by employer contributions. The aim of the scheme, the brainchild of Paul Keating, was to ensure that, as time passed, growing numbers of retirees would be able to rely on the proceeds of their superannuation savings to augment or replace their retirement income from the publicly funded age pension. The enabling legislation for the scheme was enacted in 1992.

Because of this strong focus on affordability issues, awareness of the social and psychological implications of ageing explored by Trang in her research grew quite slowly. She recalls her frustration and her efforts to stress the importance of happiness in retirement:

> I saw that everybody was talking about money, about longevity and retirement incomes and how they could be afforded. It was all about pensions, superannuation and savings, but nobody was talking about being happy, being healthy, how to adjust to new circumstances in a longer old age. I was just about the only person in those days who was talking about the psychology of ageing.
>
> I was very popular back then for giving talks at Rotary clubs and venues like that, reminding them about being happy. Telling them that, even if you are old, you must have a social network. You have to be healthy and there are other ways that you can continue to have a good and productive life by ageing well. I emphasised that these are matters of genuine concern for happiness in old age as well as superannuation, the age pensions and nursing homes.

Her appointment to head RMIT's new Applied Social Research Centre had been a major step up for Trang, one that opened the way to the top. It was an exciting and challenging time as RMIT sought to recruit senior academics to chair all of its faculties. For internal recruitment, the major criterion was that ambitious senior lecturers at or near the top of the salary scale could apply to become associate professors. Given that Trang's PhD and appointment as a senior lecturer were so recent, she was clearly not qualified to apply. Nevertheless, her dean, who was much impressed by Trang's record, advised her to apply on the grounds of special circumstances. Trang duly submitted her application. 'I was so surprised when they came back and said they would make me a full professor. I was the only woman who was appointed full professor, along with thirty-five men. I still have to laugh when I think about it because it was such a surprise outcome.'

Trang's response to her unexpected appointment was typically modest, giving little weight to her foresight in selecting an area of emerging importance as her specialty, the high quality of her academic record and her growing reputation as a researcher. No doubt her ability to bring in grant money helped her cause. In one year she raised more than a million dollars, all of it in the field of ageing, where she had little competition for funding. She was an asset of growing value to a new university whose reputation was founded in science and technology but which now sought to broaden its offerings.

Another factor made it the right time for Trang to be knocking at the door of opportunity. The 'glass ceiling' that blocked so many women from reaching the top of their professions was increasingly being challenged, with the cause of equal opportunity assisted by legislation including the Commonwealth Affirmative Action Act of 1986. Trang recalls that, because of such reforms, she was able to bring even more to her new role.

> Back then there were very few female professors in Victoria; indeed, in Australia. Even Melbourne University did not have many, and I remember that it was the start of the time when, if you were interviewing people for jobs, the panel had to be representative of both sexes. Until then there were lots of stories about females being interviewed for jobs by all-male selection panels. So the female applicants knew they would not have an equal chance. And then from somewhere this rule came into being that when universities advertised for professors, there must be a female professor involved in the selection process. And there were just so few female professors around that I was constantly being borrowed by other universities to sit on their selection panels.

There was also a significant flow-on effect right across the female workforce as anti-discrimination legislation began to bite. The feminist movement that had gathered pace in the 1970s could point with pride to the slow but inexorable erosion of inequality as male-dominated occupations were forced to review both their attitudes and the selection criteria for entry into their insular worlds.

While Trang's advancement could in many ways be regarded as a model for aspirants to higher office, she took particular pride in being a successful woman at a time when the glass ceiling, while being penetrated by increasing numbers, was still a real obstacle. In her understated but determined way she was a strong participant in the feminist cause. It is not surprising that she became one of its success stories. Driven by events and settings in which she had not been taken seriously by males, she was a strong but not strident feminist, an assertive woman quick to challenge outdated assumptions. Her daughter Elizabeth illuminates this side of Trang very well:

> She was a card carrying, flag-waving feminist from the start. I must say that she doesn't put up with anything. I remember one thing that used to happen a lot when we travelled as a family. She would travel on frequent-flyer points and her ticket was always made out to Professor Trang Thomas. The other tickets would be for Miss Elizabeth, Miss Helen and Mr David Thomas. And, whenever people looked at the tickets, they would invariably assume that Professor Thomas was my father. Mum would always make a point of correcting that. And it was interesting to see how slow people would be on the uptake. We'd have a person at the desk offering to upgrade Professor Thomas to the front and you three ladies can sit at the back. And Mum would say, 'No, no. You can put my husband at the front because he's the one with the long legs and I want to sit at the back with my daughters. And the person at the desk would say, 'That's what I said, I'll put Professor Thomas up front.' And Mum would say, 'No, no, the name on his ticket is Mr Thomas. I'm the professor but he's the one who gets the upgrade.' People would give her the strangest looks. And I must say that I always wondered why people had so much trouble with that. When I was growing up, Professor Thomas as my mother was perfectly normal. But not to others.
>
> I should also point out that while she has always been a proponent of being assertive, she tries to avoid giving offence. 'There is no need to be aggressive,' she would say. 'Everybody should look for win-win solutions.' That's how she has always approached any problem. And I think it has worked because she is so much a people person who doesn't try to make other people lose face. She is just very considerate. So that comes through and works for everybody. It's a huge strength, I think.

David, too, was extremely proud of his wife's rapid progress as an academic:

> It was huge. It not only meant that she could actually make it in the mainstream, but also that she did not have to go to a position with an ethnic orientation to be successful. It acknowledged that she was extremely bright and even being a woman in RMIT, which was basically an engineering establishment, was a big thing. She could be successful there and she was very happy with that.

Impressive as it was, Trang's professional success was only the precursor to greater things. Like a butterfly emerging from its mature chrysalis, her wings had unfolded to dry in the sun and had been tested as she broke through the glass ceiling. The 1990s would be her time to fly high.

Trang Thomas, PhD, La Trobe University, 1989.

Trang with teenage daughters Helen and Elizabeth, 1990.

- CHAPTER 26 -

Political Engagement

Delhi, January 2015

For even such a seasoned traveller as Trang, waking to a new day in Delhi was a unique experience. She knew that it was one of the world's largest cities and that it incorporated the territory of New Delhi, the national capital. She had expected crowded streets and the restless energy of the struggle for subsistence that is the enduring image of India, but was unprepared for the avalanche of vehicles that emerged blindly from the morning fog to swamp every street, lane and rubbish-strewn alley. Within minutes, a million foot soldiers joined the mechanised ranks of the swarm to begin the day's myriad activities of work and survival. Trang watched and listened intently as their cries joined the unceasing clamour of horns to signal that Delhi was open for business.

Robyn and I also watched with great interest from the vantage point of our fourth-floor hotel window. A tour of India had not been on our bucket list, but Trang had been persuasive. 'This is not a professional development tour,' she had assured Robyn. 'It is a holiday. You will both enjoy a break and there will be plenty of opportunities to record more information for my biography.' So we had come in the Indian winter to fog-bound Delhi, looking forward to exploring the huge city before making our way south through Rajasthan to spend time in Mumbai and Goa.

By then I was accustomed to ad hoc interviews with Trang in distant locations, a pleasing blend of purpose and our mutual enjoyment of travel. 'This time I'd like to talk about the early 1990s,' I told her. 'That was when you took leave from your busy post as RMIT University's first female professor to immerse yourself in broader society. I'm looking forward to learning how that came about.'

'Of course,' she agreed. 'I took the first steps on my own initiative and, from that beginning, a lot of opportunities came my way because I was in the right place at the right time. I still look back in disbelief at some of the appointments I took on.'

Melbourne, 1991-92

David's venture into politics had nothing to do with money, as he had to take a large reduction in salary to make the change. His major task as the Liberal opposition's economics advisor was to develop economic reform policies for the party to take to the four-yearly Victorian election due in 1992. It was a very challenging time. David was on his own, striving to respond to the Labor government's initiatives while continuing to develop alternative policies for the opposition. It says much for his skills that he managed to stay on the front foot until the 1992 election, a landslide win to the Liberals that brought Jeff Kennett to the Premier's office. Soon after achieving his objective, David returned to Swinburne. But the cut and thrust of politics never left him and in the years to come he remained involved.

David's decision to throw his weight behind the Victorian Liberals exposed his family to political issues and sparked their awareness of current affairs. He recalled that Elizabeth and Helen became interested in his work:

> They used to watch the news to see what was happening in the political debate. So they became more informed and worldly than you might expect at that age. But they were otherwise just your usual kids. They learned swimming, dancing and piano. I think they had a reasonably normal upbringing but I couldn't swear to that, not really knowing what normal means.

Trang, too, felt the call of political involvement. Despite her strong focus on research during her quick rise to the senior academic ranks, she made time in the early 1990s to take a more active interest in both politics and the broader community area of ethnic affairs. Melbourne was of course strongly multicultural by then. Its ethnic communities were well established and not slow to speak out on issues relevant to their interests. The Vietnamese community in particular was already aware of Trang's achievements and her potential to be a strong representative voice.

She found a way to get involved in politics without interrupting unduly her busy work schedule. Some years previously, Lorraine Elliott, wife of Liberal Party identity John Elliott, had established a women's group to encourage women interested in Liberal politics to have a voice. Lorraine recalled the origins of the group:

> I had joined with another woman in starting a women's section of the Liberal Party that met in the evenings. That was unusual. Most such groups met during the day, and I could see that many women who were working couldn't attend those meetings. Meanwhile the Labor Party had their Emily's List, led mainly by Joan Kirner and some other prominent feminists. They'd been promoting the Labor Party as the party for women, so we began this women's section, which had a silly name really: the Canterbury Women's Discussion Group. But it was successful in attracting women, several of whom went on to become parliamentary representatives.
>
> The group was well established when Trang decided to join. I don't remember clearly the occasion, but she said later that when she came I was very welcoming. I guess it was a big step for her, because it was largely an Anglo-background group. Several of the women in that group have remained close friends, so my friendship with Trang just grew organically out of that original political connection.

Trang had mixed feelings about joining the group. A friend and colleague who encouraged her was Kay Patterson, an academic she had met at a number of psychology conferences before Kay became a senator and eventually Federal Minister for Health. Trang recalls that she remained unsure about whether she would fit in:

> Kay Patterson said to me: 'Why don't you just come along?' But I hesitated before eventually deciding to attend. In my mind, I didn't seem to fit the Liberal Party image of women who wore suits and had to have their hair done to go to that sort of meeting. But when I went to the group they were so nice, especially Lorraine, so easygoing. Very,

> very natural and very warm. So I felt as though I belonged and that I would contribute in whatever way I could. And there was an obvious way. There were politicians in marginal seats where there were many Asian constituents, so I said I'd come along with them, walking the streets and meeting the people, and help out. There weren't many Asian people in the Liberal Party in those days. So I could translate for the candidates, assist with materials, including letters in Vietnamese, and that was a help.

David recalled Trang's participation in the Victorian Liberal Party's state election campaign in 1992:

> Trang's support for the Liberals was to some degree the fallout from her rather unsatisfactory experience with the great Gough when her folks were boat people. When she joined the Liberal women's group, she became a supporter of certain Liberal Party politicians, including Michael Wooldridge, the member for Chisholm. His seat, which he had won from Labour in 1988, included parts of Box Hill, a suburb with a very substantial number of Asian immigrants. Trang was by then becoming fairly well known among the multicultural community. Having her walking through the Vietnamese quarter and talking to them, introducing him, was good for Michael. I don't know whether it garnered him many votes but I think it probably did. And it was a very marginal seat.

Trang's support role for Michael Wooldridge was not a formal appointment, just something she did as a personal contribution to the party. She and Lorraine Elliott became very close friends, a relationship that was sustained until Lorraine's untimely death in mid-2014. Both would go on to make their marks in their chosen professions. Lorraine won the Victorian Legislative Assembly seat of Mooroolbark in the 1992 election that saw Jeff Kennett become Premier. She retained her seat for ten years, becoming parliamentary secretary for both the Arts and Community Services during 1999–2002. Following her parliamentary career, she remained active in politics and community affairs. Lorraine developed a keen appreciation for the qualities Trang brought to both her work and her friendships:

Trang has always been a very interesting person. I think most Australians don't know someone from a different background who they can say is really their friend. The two of us are close, so I can tease her or whatever. Trang and I have had our children growing up at the same time and we've had our ups and downs, not the same things happening but a shared experience. And we've seen our children become adults and our friendship has stayed very strong during that time. David was part of that friendship, of course.

Joining the discussion group was a big step for Trang. But, because Trang is also a feminist, I think she was looking for a women's group and ours suited her political inclinations. I think, too, that she has somehow been very good at having a foot in both the Australian and the Vietnamese communities. She has always done that extremely well. And I think she's been a real pioneer in many ways, bridging the gaps between communities. When I went to Alice Springs, there was Trang featured in the Pioneer Women's Museum. She was the first female Professor at RMIT and certainly the first Vietnamese. She's broken through a lot of glass ceilings. And the thing I've always found about Trang and what I've tried to learn from her is that she has that Buddhist air of calm. For example, her family has suffered terribly but she has that Buddhist air of calm acceptance. Sort of 'life is like that', and she doesn't seem to get angry or resentful.

Trang's growing interest and involvement in politics eventually led to a dilemma. Should she nominate for political office or stay with the academic career path that was serving her so well? But much would happen before she confronted that decision. The incoming Kennett government introduced legislation that brought an opportunity to serve in a quasi-political role, a chance she embraced because it offered another way to make a difference.

- CHAPTER 27 -

Victorian Multicultural Commission

Melbourne, 1994-97

Among the Kennett government's early legislative changes was a completely new Ethnic Affairs Act. That in turn led to the vacancy for a suitable person to chair the Victorian Ethnic Affairs Commission (VEAC), soon to be renamed the Victorian Multicultural Commission (VMC). As a commission, it was an independent body, which meant that there was scope for a creative approach. Trang had immediately been attracted to the job. Her family supported her decision to apply for the vacancy so she went ahead. Financial self-interest played no part in her decision. The salary offered for the post of Commissioner was actually less than her professorial salary at RMIT. It was just an exciting and challenging time and she wanted very much to be a part of change for the better in a society adapting, at times with misgivings, to new ideas and imperatives.

Trang's application involved her in the usual competitive process: interviews and shortlisting leading to her eventual selection. Her appointment attracted much more attention from the media than she'd modestly expected. There were good reasons, not least that she was breaking new ground as a female Asian immigrant. When her appointment was announced, she was inundated by requests for media interviews. It helped that she had just completed her research project, *New Land, Last Home*, for the Bureau of Immigration and Population Research. The book was launched by Premier Jeff Kennett at Parliament House and that, too, had attracted media attention. Then, while she was settling in to her appointment, her successful mediation of the heated conflict between the Greek and Macedonian communities raised her public profile to new heights. Journalists, impressed by her background and demonstrated capabilities, continued to give her exposure throughout her four-year term. Their attention was reinforced by her ability to provide clear and succinct answers to questions put to her about contentious issues. She smiles at the memory of her popularity with the media:

> It was hard on my boss, the minister assisting the premier for ethnic affairs. Always photos of me and not of him. There was a journalist who specialised in ethnic affairs in the newspaper and he praised me for being so accessible. One thing I learned very early in public office was that you should always be available to the journalists. And, if you appear arrogant, then the next time they will not ask you.

At age forty-seven, Trang could hardly believe that almost thirty years had passed since she had arrived in Australia to take up her scholarship at UNSW. Now that she had enjoyed academic success, the restlessness of spirit that unfailingly drove her to new challenges had well and truly resurfaced. During her almost two decades at RMIT, she had risen to the top tier but there was much more to be explored in a society, long since embraced as her own, that was experiencing immense social and economic change, including steady progress towards the broad acceptance of multiculturalism as the natural order. It was time now to explore the ideas and tentative plans she had brought to her new appointment, her first outside the field of tertiary education.

As it happened, much was already happening to engage her attention. On the national scene, an influx of Cambodian, Vietnamese and Chinese refugees prompted the Keating government to introduce mandatory detention for asylum seekers. Under the new legislation, all persons entering Australia without a valid visa would be detained and possibly subject to deportation. The new border security measures reminded her of the aftermath of the fall of Saigon in 1975 and the tragic loss of her family members that followed. In her home state of Victoria, there were many other issues for her to address among the almost two hundred ethnic groups served by the VMC. With the wry grin that her friends love, she recalls the multiple demands of her position:

My primary role was to promote harmony among the communities. It is impossible to please everyone, of course, so I operated on that premise. It was like working with two hundred mothers-in-law. And I had to take in my stride the many cultural differences among groups, such as the concept of time. On one occasion I was invited to an ethnic community dinner to begin at 7pm. I arrived but no one was there. The venue was in darkness. Finally, I decided that I must have somehow mistaken the day and I was about to go home when some people arrived to begin setting up the tables. The dinner eventually started at 9pm. No one seemed to find that strange at all.

Funding for community initiatives was very competitive and, for Trang the feminist, discussion of applications for grants was often challenging in light of traditional attitudes to women. She recalls being welcomed by an assembly of students when she attended a school for discussions. She was surprised to find all of the boys sitting in the front rows of the assembly hall, while the girls all sat at the back. She asked why and was told that the girls' education was far less important. So she told the community leaders in no uncertain terms that this was definitely not the way to support their case for extra funding. On another occasion she funded a book for Muslim women, about cultural attitudes and the injustice of having their rights and acceptable activities determined by men. As a feminist, she felt proud to be helping a group to try to change discriminatory attitudes and practices within their own culture. There were certainly many issues to address. Shortly after, she was visited by a group of male community leaders to discuss project funding. They refused to shake her hand because she was a woman. 'This is me,' she told them sternly. 'This is what you get. I'm the only person here for you to speak with. If you persist with that kind of attitude, I might have to consider your request for funding in a broader context.'

In her own assertive way, Trang thus combined her skills as a psychologist and her propensity to question entrenched attitudes to negotiate mutually respectful outcomes with men. Once they learned that she would not put up with their attitudes to women, they would be much more careful to meet her respect with theirs. She was never heavy-handed, preferring to leave space for pragmatic attitudinal adjustment without serious loss of face.

Interestingly, Trang's role as the public face of ethnic affairs also taught her that her staff took her growing influence and media exposure very seriously. Her image was very important to them. Trang herself was not one to be overly concerned about keeping up appearances. 'I had to make adjustments,' she recalls.

> For example, I like to wear pants. They are comfortable for work and that is important to me on the job. But there was one time when I had agreed to a request for press photographs and I was told by one of my staff that I should go home and change into a dress. Being interviewed and photographed by the press was considered to be a formal occasion, I suppose. I learned from that, and ever since I have always kept a change of clothing in the workplace. A suit, stockings and high heels.

While her new position was a demanding and often thankless appointment, it brought rewards that she welcomed. In late 1993, one of her more pleasant tasks, and one dear to her heart, was to lay the foundation stone for the only residential care facility for elderly Vietnamese in Melbourne. She had helped the community to obtain a permit for the facility. Her contribution was not forgotten. In January 2014, she was invited to a function there to celebrate the Year of the Horse, and learned that the Victorian government had just provided $8 million to extend the residence.

Trang's growing academic profile and elevation to her key role in ethnic affairs brought unexpected recognition. In 1994, UNSW recognised Trang's growing list of achievements by including her in its annual distinguished alumni awards. Since their commencement in 1972, the awards have gone to alumni who have made outstanding contributions to the community, who have stimulated new ideas and services and who have exhibited exceptional dedication, creativity or leadership. Trang had joined a distinguished company of achievers. She was surprised and honoured by her award and, ever conscious of her role in the encouragement of multiculturalism, she expressed her pleasure at its significance in recognising ethnic women and their contribution to Australian society.

Recognition of her achievements encouraged her to keep pressing for reforms to services for migrants from non-English speaking background (NESB), especially the aged. She made a notable breakthrough in this area during her time as Commissioner by establishing an inquiry into government services for migrants, in particular the aged living in ethnic communities. Drawing on her own research expertise in the area of ageing, she set up a project team to collect data in the field, then analysed the data to identify the areas in which reform was most needed. The inquiry came up with a comprehensive report including 160 recommendations, many of which were accepted and implemented by the Victorian government. It was a very satisfying outcome that once more demonstrated the innovative ideas, skills and determination she had brought to the appointment. David recalled that Trang was often asked, 'How can you work with someone like Jeff Kennett? He's such a big and impatient fellow.' Her response reflected her self-confident outlook. 'Everyone is bigger than I am. If I worried about that I'd never get anything done.'

There was yet another aspect to her appointment to her VMC role that would broaden her experience immensely. Her subsequent exposure through the media brought requests that she could never have foreseen. The first came from Foreign Minister Gareth Evans.

Victorian Ethnic Affairs Commissioner, Professor Trang Thomas, discusses her successful mediation of the Greek-Macedonian dispute with TV and print journalists, 1994.

Proud recipient Trang with her Distinguished Alumni Award from UNSW, 1994.

- CHAPTER 28 -

Trang Goes International

Melbourne, 1994-95

The call from Foreign Minister Evans surprised Trang. Still busily assessing the scope of her multicultural responsibilities, she had not anticipated early requests to take part in broader representational activities, let alone as a member of Australia's committee for the United Nations' fiftieth anniversary. While the task would add to her already heavy workload, she felt she could not refuse because it appealed to her sense of being an Australian citizen. But why her? She decided that her invitation to participate came primarily because she ticked three of the right boxes as an ethnic female professor. So she agreed and thanked the Foreign Minister for his invitation.

While the UN anniversary was in 1995, more than a year away, Trang was sure that Evans would push hard for early initiatives. He was not one for waiting patiently for something to happen. The first full committee meeting was held in Canberra on 3 February 1994. Senator Evans announced that Australia would play a leading role in commemoration activities because the nation's ambassador to the UN, Richard Butler, had been elected as chair of the UN's own preparatory committee. It was clear that Senator Evans expected Australia to set a high standard. He explained that a key aim of the anniversary celebrations was to increase community awareness and understanding of the world body and its initiatives. Accordingly, the committee would provide advice on appropriate government activities, as well as working with the broader community to plan and publicise a range of non-government initiatives. Trang recalls the planning procedures and public-speaking engagements:

The committee met monthly. It was clear that we would have to talk to a large number of people across Australia, so a lot of travel would be involved. We divided the publicity task among the members, so I would go to regional cities like Cairns and Townsville to tell people about the UN, describing Australia's role and promoting it as a vital organisation for global action on many fronts, including resettlement of refugees and the promotion of human rights. For me, it was an enjoyable experience because I met many very interesting groups of people and learned a surprising amount myself. I was not to know it at the time, but what I learned was most relevant to my later experience with the rights of refugees.

Senator Evans must have appreciated Trang's initial contribution. He called her again when, later in 1994, he sent a delegation to Vietnam to investigate the communist regime's treatment of ethnic groups. Much of the pressure on the Australian government to carry out the investigation came from allegations by Vietnamese communities in Australia of abuse of human rights in their former home. Given that Vietnam was still quite closed to the outside world, it was a politically charged decision by the Australian government to send the delegation. Its acceptance by Vietnam was perhaps an acknowledgement of the strong support by elements of Australia's political left for North Vietnam's victory in 1975. The Whitlam government had been quick to recognise the new regime and equally quick to discourage the notion that Australia, as a participant in the conflict, should take in Vietnamese refugees. Hence Trang's strong reaction when her appeal for help for her parents was refused. Given that experience, she was quite surprised when the Foreign Minister of the Keating Labor government called her in person to find out if she was prepared to join the delegation.

Trang was aware that the regime in Vietnam had in recent years begun to acknowledge that broad reforms to its authoritarian society might be necessary. The forced unification of the nation had not brought the communist utopia foreseen by Ho Chi Minh and his followers. Disaffection, isolation and poverty had taken a heavy toll on the new regime's credibility and the economy was a basket case. With a new determination to engage with the West, sensitive issues, including that of human rights, were no longer off the diplomatic table. While still unwilling to deal with United

Nations agencies, the Vietnamese government was prepared to enter into discussions with a small number of countries, including Australia. Trang was not optimistic about the outcome of the delegation's efforts. 'But it is a start,' she told herself. 'I will accept the offer and contribute whatever I can.' So she told Senator Evans that she would be pleased to join the delegation.

Given the political sensitivities involved, the purpose and scope of the delegation's activities had to be framed in an acceptable way that avoided offence to or loss of face by Vietnamese officials. It was a very special concession to be allowed into the country, especially since the delegation would be accompanied by an ABC news team.

The delegation duly followed its itinerary. In Trang's opinion, the whole trip was an exercise in window-dressing.

> Alexander Downer and Stephen Loosley were team leaders. So the group of experts in various aspects of Vietnam was led by a representative group of politicians. Everywhere we went, the Vietnamese officials showed us centres where they were supposed to be training women to give them jobs. Things like that. We would look at them, but it was all a sham. That was understandable. After all, why would they let us see anything else? Why would they let a group of foreigners come in to inspect their work? Clearly they wanted to project a favourable image, but that was all. On another occasion, we went to the Buddhist temple in Hue where there were some dissident monks. On the day of the visit, all of the monks were sent away on a 'picnic'. Only a few young novices were there, so we were unable to conduct any interviews.
>
> The ABC followed and filmed us to send stories back to Australia on how the delegation was progressing. It wasn't good coverage at all. They filmed us drinking wine with Vietnamese officials. They portrayed the whole trip as a junket undertaken to appease our Australian Vietnamese community.

While Trang was disappointed with the outcome, she enjoyed an unexpected bonus. While in North Vietnam, she was able to visit an uncle to get news of extended-family members who had remained behind after Ho's victory against the French. Her uncle organised a family reunion for the occasion.

She was also able to visit her beloved nanny, who had married after Trang's departure from Hanoi in 1954 and had her own children and grandchildren. Trang was visibly moved when she spoke about the meeting:

> She was so happy to see me. Over the years I had sent her money to help out when she needed it. She has since died, of course. She was old by then. But I've never forgotten that she was the very first influence on my life in a household where nobody else seemed to have much interest in me. I was the apple of her eye. I was so glad that she later married and had her own life.

In 1995, Trang was again asked to join a delegation, this time to China. The delegation, led by eminent Victorian jurist Sir James Gobbo, was tasked to observe China's progress towards better treatment of its substantial minorities. The visit was another building block towards closer relations with the emerging giant. There has been a regular exchange of delegations between the two countries since that time. For Trang, the visit was another part of the learning curve that enhanced her understanding of multicultural and human rights issues in Australia and Asia. The valuable experience she gained from these representations to Australia's neighbours undoubtedly helped to make her a go-to person for inclusion on councils and committees created by successive federal governments to engage the broader population.

Despite her strong commitment to work and community, Trang was deeply conscious of her family responsibilities and her current reliance on David's unfailing support and commitment. He, too, was engaged in public representation in addition to his position at Swinburne University. Not surprisingly, the call of politics had remained strong and another opportunity arose in 1994 when, in the eastern suburbs of Melbourne, the City of Boroondara was created from the amalgamation of Kew, Camberwell and Hawthorn. David was appointed as one of three commissioners of the new city, serving for three years until the amalgamation was complete and elections for the city council could be called. He was particularly proud of his role as commissioner. The competing demands of university, city administration and support for his family, as Trang coped with the multiple demands of her appointments, kept him very busy indeed.

As an exhausting 1995 came to an end, Trang looked forward to a

Christmas break with family and friends. She needed the time off to regroup, sensing that 1996 would stretch further the boundaries of her contribution to national and community affairs, multiculturalism and the advancement of women in general. It seemed a long time since she had undertaken PhD studies to enhance her academic career prospects.

Trang represents Australia in Federal Parliamentary Delegation to Vietnam, April 1995. Meeting with the Archbishop of Hanoi.

Trang with eminent jurist Sir James Gobbo, Federal Parliamentary Human Rights Delegation to China, 1995.

- CHAPTER 29 -

The Prime Minister Calls

Melbourne, 1996-97

'For you, Trang.' Trang took the phone, wondering who had tracked her down. She had been out of her office for much of the day, and had made time to attend an afternoon meeting of women hosted by her friend Jenny Rawther (now Russell). She was surprised to find herself speaking to Prime Minister John Howard's office. Then a new voice came on the line.

'I've called to offer the best gig going in Australia right now,' John Howard said. 'I'd like you to serve on the Council for the Centenary of Federation.'

Trang was momentarily speechless. She quickly rallied, accepting the appointment and inviting him to say hello to the others. He agreed cheerfully, so she turned to the ladies. 'It's the Prime Minister,' she said. 'Would you like to say hello?'

'Oh, yes!' her friends chorused. 'Of course we would. Who else would it be? Good one, Trang.'

It was indeed an honour to be offered the opportunity to participate in a national celebration. The Council, to be chaired by entrepreneur and aviation identity Dick Smith and including representatives from each state and territory, would be tasked to develop a nationwide program of events to celebrate the centenary in 2001. Hence the PM's unexpected call to Trang to offer her a place as a representative of the federal government.

She struggled to come fully to grips with the turn of events. The holder of Australia's highest political office had called personally to recruit her to a position of great honour. Why her? As usual, her first thought was that the offer was yet another case of the 'three birds with one stone' advantage of being an ethnic female professor, now with the added attraction of relevant experience to ward off suggestions of tokenism or political patronage. 'People always tell me that it's not that at all,' she says. 'They assure me that I received these appointments on merit only. But I'm sure that it wasn't just one thing or the other. There must have been a "right time, right place" element as well as any consideration of merit.'

Whatever the weighting given to her various attributes, Trang was delighted at her inclusion on the Council. 'It was a real love job. Perhaps by that time I shouldn't have been quite so astonished, because I'd been approached before by senior officeholders. So I was already quite well known.'

The VMC issued a press release on 4 December 1996 to announce Trang's new appointment. The details included her response to her nomination:

> It is a great honour for me to be on this Council. The Centenary of Federation will be an occasion for all of us to show our pride in the achievements of our country. We shall celebrate the many cultures in Australia and our achieving harmony in diversity. I would like all Australians, regardless of being Australian born or foreign born, living in regional or urban areas, to have the opportunities of joining in the celebrations and showing that they are proud of being Australian.

The press release went on to compliment Trang on her philosophy of hard work and self-reliance, instilled in her by her mother, noting that it had been an extraordinary rise for a woman who was born Vu Thi Ngoc Trang near the Vietnamese city of Hanoi, later fleeing to Saigon with her parents to escape communism before coming to Australia a decade later.

Christmas 1996 was once more a welcome break, a time for Trang to set aside her full schedule to focus on her all-important family. David too was happy to slow down for a few days. Elizabeth and Helen were now young women pursuing their own goals. But the relative quiet of midsummer January presaged yet another surprise recognition of their mother's achievements. The 1997 Australia Day Honours List included Professor Ngoc Trang Thomas as a Member of the Order of Australia (AM). Her award acknowledged her leading contribution to research into the issues of ageing and her already impressive record as chair of the Victorian Multicultural Commission.

Trang duly attended her investiture at Government House, where Victorian Governor Richard McGarvie officiated. She had met McGarvie previously, and had great respect for him. Given the importance of the Governor's role in public relations, it had been one of her many duties to visit his office with members of the Multicultural Commission to discuss ways and means of fostering closer relations among the ethnic communities.

She was keenly conscious of the significance of the honour, listening and watching intently as the citations of her fellow recipients were read and one by one they moved up to receive their awards. She recalls a humorous moment when Stephen Seif, a leader of the Egyptian community, was recognised for 'helping the ethnic communities to pay their taxes'. 'There was a lot of laughter when that was read out,' she said. 'What they meant was that he'd done lot to educate the communities about the Australian taxation system.'

Trang had barely recovered from the surprise of her AM when, in early 1997, the Council for the Centenary of Federation began its deliberations. It was a task that would engage her in detailed planning activities over the following four years. In addition to Dick Smith and herself, the disparate group of representatives of the federal government were celebrity entertainer 'Angry' Anderson, Indigenous tennis legend Evonne Goolagong, church leader Peter Hollingworth, later to be appointed Governor-General, and distinguished historian Geoffrey Blainey.

Together with representatives from the states and territories, the group would meet regularly to plan the celebrations with a budget of $300 million for facilities and events around the nation. Projects included such items as the development of Federation Square in Victoria and a huge float on the Brisbane River in Queensland. 'It was an exciting time,' says Trang. 'It brought home to me more than ever that, for an immigrant as much as anyone else, anything was possible in this country. And there was an added bonus. 'With all of that money to be allocated, I suddenly found that I had a lot of new friends.'

The task also had its lighter moments. Trang remembers appearing on the program *This is Your Life*. The episode featured the chair, Dick Smith.

The producers wanted to film him, but as always it was planned as a surprise. So they arranged with the Council to film one of our meetings. It couldn't be done in our usual meeting room, so the venue was changed to one of the hotels where there was more space. There was a large window and the film crew would be on the other side of the room filming our meeting. We were told beforehand that something was going to happen but we didn't know what it would be. So it was an unexpected moment for Dick when he was presented with his book, *This is Your Life*, during the meeting. He was genuinely surprised. And it was great for us all to see how the show was produced.

One would have thought that Trang had enough on her plate with her ethnic affairs job and planning for the Centenary of Federation. That was not to be. Within months, in August 1997, she felt another strong tap on her shoulder. Victorian Premier Jeff Kennett asked her to serve on the board of the newly legislated Casino and Gaming Authority. The casino in Melbourne had just been built and was about to open, necessitating an upgrade to state regulatory arrangements for gaming. It was a five-year appointment and Trang was quite surprised to be asked.

I am not a gambler and I didn't even want to know about the industry. I remember that when I was asked I cried because I just didn't want to be involved in anything to do with gambling. Can you imagine that? But I was told that I was needed in the job because the casino would have a large number of Asian customers. The government felt that it would be good to have someone with a good understanding of Asian cultures. I was told that, if I didn't accept, they would have to look for another Asian person. So I let myself be persuaded.

With her strong reservations still battling her sense of obligation, Trang was duly appointed. There was, however, an immediate benefit. She remembers the opening of the casino as an amazing night. 'As a Board member, I was on the A-list. We were sitting there being serenaded by singers Anthony Warlow and Kylie Minogue and watching the best ever fireworks display.' It was fortunate that she enjoyed the occasion so much, because her participation for the next five years offered little else in the way of entertainment.

The Board did not hear every matter, of course. The Casino and Gaming Authority had support staff: a CEO and experts in the different compliance areas. Their responsibilities included routine checking on compliance with standards required from operators of gaming facilities, including poker machines, and response to complaints about venues or operations. Such matters were referred to the Board only when unusually difficult or contentious circumstances arose. Trang recalls one issue of great concern to her:

> I found the issue of problem gambling very troubling. There were all sorts of stories about how gambling tore families apart, about addicted parents becoming so indebted that suicide seemed the only way out. There was a very strong anti-gambling group. To them, everything the casino did was bad. All the time such negative stories, and questions were sometimes referred to the Board. But there was little that we could do to help individuals who got themselves into real trouble.

Because Trang was so well known to the media, she was often approached for comment on controversial matters. She found the interviews quite daunting and, not surprisingly, would worry about her presentation. David, by now accustomed to her numerous appointments, was supportive as always, making a practice of taping her TV interviews so that she could review them later. She learned quite a lot from that process. Nevertheless, she was grateful when her term was over, and she has not darkened the doors of the casino, or indeed any other gaming venue, since then. She does not even buy lottery tickets.

Busy as she was, Trang was keenly aware that her four-year term at the VMC was coming to an end. That in turn meant that she was faced with a dilemma. Should she seek to renew her appointment, or should she return to her professorial duties at RMIT? The university had been very supportive in giving her four years' leave of absence, but now it was time for her to go back or resign. She weighed up her choices with great care. Her present job was exciting and challenging. There was no doubt that her work during the past four years had been a major contribution to the cause of multiculturalism in Australia. On the other hand, her RMIT position offered tenure and stability. And she loved the job. She could speak her mind without being constrained by politics, and she missed her young students and her research work. On balance, she decided that the best option was to return to RMIT.

Despite Trang's sound reasons for leaving the VMC, her departure was a wrench. Her time there had raised her profile and brought widespread respect for her abilities. And while she had achieved much in the provision of adequate and appropriate services for migrants, she had also stressed consistently that the grant of Australian citizenship conferred not only rights and entitlements, but also the obligation of loyalty and respect for the nation's legal and sociocultural institutions. But there were always undercurrents of resistance to the concept of multiculturalism, and she was saddened by the surge of public support for federal political newcomer Pauline Hanson's hard-line stance on Asian immigration. She felt that it was a significant backwards step in community relations. On her departure, Trang commented that she looked forward to the day when Australia no longer needed such commissions or equal opportunity boards because cultural diversity would be accepted as normal.

That was and remains Trang's dream, a vision dancing before her like an ever-receding mirage. Unfortunately, many of the events of the twenty-first century to date have not been conducive to unqualified acceptance of the principles she expressed so convincingly. The advent of global terrorism and increased flows of refugees from the world's conflict zones have sparked strong debate in Australia and other Western nations. Trang herself would become closely involved with related issues, including the human rights of asylum seekers. But, before then, she would find herself juggling many more community obligations because of her strong sense of duty, coupled with the drive that made her unable to say no to a challenge.

CHAPTER 29 - The Prime Minister Calls

Helen, Trang and David enjoying Egypt, 1996.

Premier Jeff Kennett outlines the Victorian Government's response to the Inquiry into Services for Elderly Immigrants led by Trang, 1996-97.

Trang with close friend, Victorian parliamentarian Lorraine Elliott, at Lorraine's marriage to journalist and newspaper editor John Kiely, Melbourne 1996.

- CHAPTER 30 -

Trang and the Special Broadcasting Service

Melbourne, 1997-99

The years of Trang's transition from the VMC back to her professorial duties would see her maintain her high-level involvement in community affairs. They also brought loss and grief. Mother died in the United States in July 1998, where she had spent her final years living with her son Dzi. Her passing was a great blow to Trang, who received the news while completing a trip to Vietnam for a psychology conference. It was hard for her to accept that the most influential woman among a select group who had steered her personal development, values and professional aspirations was gone. Sadly, she returned to her multifaceted life and career, facing the reality that she and her siblings were now the oldest generation of her family. She wondered how she, the expert on ageing issues, would cope with becoming an older Australian. A sobering thought, but one that was quickly lost in the need to keep up the frenetic pace she now regarded as normal.

Soon after, she was approached to undertake a task that would make good use of her experience in ethnic affairs. This time the call came from Federal Minister for Communications Richard Alston. There was a vacancy on the board of the Special Broadcasting Service (SBS) that he would like her to fill.

The minister's request was not surprising. Trang was already familiar with the SBS. Established in 1980 to provide ethnic communities with access to news and programs directly related to their countries of origin, the service had underlined the emerging commitment to multiculturalism under the Fraser governments from 1975 to 1983. It followed the acceptance of large numbers of Vietnamese refugees from the late 1970s and others fleeing from conflicts in the Middle East. By the late 1990s, Trang was well known for her ongoing representation of ethnic communities in their requests for more cultural and linguistic diversity in the programs provided by SBS. Despite its obvious appeal to its target communities, many immigrants were not satisfied with the service's initial offerings. Trang explains:

> The SBS always did a good job for the ethnic communities through its radio broadcasting service. The broadcasts in different languages were particularly well received. But the television side was lacking. It brought in all sorts of exotic movies for Australians, for example, but the feeling was that it wasn't doing enough. It has since improved a lot. If you tune in now, in the mornings they prepare and present news from various countries in their own languages. That content was previously brought in from the countries concerned, an expedient practice but one that didn't always attract a positive response. Some of the ethnic groups did not favour the current governments in their countries of origin. For example, the Vietnamese were quite disaffected by what they saw as government propaganda. The radio news was different. It was prepared in Australia using Australian commentators. But not the television news. We had a demonstration if front of SBS with the demonstrators calling for the program's removal. 'We don't want it,' they said. So to this day the SBS does not broadcast Vietnamese news on television.

Despite her high profile and understanding of the issues, it was a difficult decision for Trang to accept a position on the SBS Board of Directors. She was reluctant to add to her already full schedule. On the other hand, she was moved to accept the appointment because she was an obvious choice to represent multicultural interests. It was also a critical time for the public broadcaster. There was talk of amalgamation with the Australian Broadcasting Commission (ABC). Why have two separate public broadcasters when one could do it all?

The issue was strongly debated, with the ethnic communities firmly behind the retention of an independent SBS. Meanwhile, Trang was learning quickly about SBS's shoestring budget and the art of funding locally produced projects with few resources. SBS was so poor that, to set up and conduct an interview, it could spend only about $100 per minute in contrast to the

ABC's $300 per minute and up to $3000 for the commercial channels. The latter had much greater resources, of course, because of their advertising revenue. They could afford to fund expensive, Australian-produced soaps, like the popular *Home and Away*, while the SBS bought cheaper programs from overseas.

There was an amusing response to some of the imported content. Many European television productions were quite risqué by Australian broadcasting standards. Viewers offended by graphic sex scenes would complain to Trang that SBS was a pornographic channel. Conversely, others complained that SBS showed its pornographic content too late at night. It just wasn't the best time for them. As always, Trang took the complaints in her stride:

> It showed once more that you can't please everybody. But you have to do your best for your audience. We used a lot of psychology on the Board. For example, when the ratings were down we had to change programs. We knew from experience that programs about Napoleon and Hitler were always popular, so we would show those. Those guys were just such an attraction, despite one of them being very evil. But that's human nature, isn't it? We are fascinated by strong people. And then there was *South Park*. Young people in the eighteen to twenty-five age range didn't watch so much TV, and certainly not SBS. But we were able to buy *South Park* and they loved it. Our ratings for that time slot went through the roof.

The business of running SBS aside, Trang found it engaging and informative to meet and hear the views of SBS presenters like Margaret Pomeranz and David Stratton. Sometimes they would lunch with the Board members, along with news and current affairs favourites Indira Naidoo, Lee Lin Chin, Mary Kostakidis and Jana Wendt. 'Having lunch with celebrities and gaining insight from their experiences was something outside the norm for us,' she recalls fondly. 'The Board members also got along well. When I first attended, the President gave me a treat by taking me for a ride in her Rolls-Royce.'

The threat of amalgamation with the ABC did not eventuate. Trang's major focus during her time on the Board was therefore the refinement and expansion of TV services along the lines requested by the ethnic communities. Her advocacy for this outcome is another example of her capacity to advocate for innovative changes to current policy and practice. Inevitably, her successes further raised her profile, strengthening her appeal as the go-to person for community service appointments that required both expertise and strong initiative.

'What next?' she wondered as she worked hard at fitting in her new commitments while preparing to re-engage with her academic career at RMIT. The answer soon arrived. She was encouraged by Liberal Party friends and supporters to compete for preselection for a Senate seat at the 1998 federal election. Having just resolved one dilemma, she was faced with another. If successful, she would become the first Asian candidate to be elected to that body. Given her strong belief in equality of representation and her obvious credentials, the opportunity was compelling. On the other hand, she had looked forward her return to RMIT. Ever adventurous, and strongly encouraged by David, she decided to throw her hat into the political ring. In the event, her bid for preselection was unsuccessful. Typically, she was quite philosophical about the divided loyalties and machinations of party politics that determined the final outcome. She took the positive view that her academic path was once more clear, and there would be more opportunities for valuable community service to provide interesting and challenging diversions.

- CHAPTER 31 -

Constitutional Convention

Canberra, 1997-99

Almost inevitably, even as Trang focused on her future and her SBS appointment, yet another very special task came her way. The Howard government announced that a constitutional convention would be held to discuss the issue of whether Australia should remain a constitutional monarchy or become a republic. Who better than Trang could be chosen to represent multicultural interests?

The debate on whether Australia should become a republic instead of a constitutional monarchy had intensified following a speech by Prime Minister Paul Keating in June 1995. He expressed his strong support for Australia to be led by an Australian and that the change from a constitutional monarchy to a republic should be achieved by 2001, the centenary of federation.

Feelings ran high between staunch royalists and avowed republicans. It was a debate about a complex and far-reaching proposal to address a situation that was anachronistic and often puzzling for other nations in their dealings with Australia. While many Australian citizens supported the republican viewpoint, just as many did not see the issue as a problem that needed a resolution, because Australia had long been an independent nation. Well, almost. For them, a popular argument against change was, 'If it ain't broke, don't fix it.'

Keating lost power to the Howard government in 1996, but the debate continued to gain momentum and it was clearly time for the issue to be addressed by the federal parliament. Accordingly, in March 1997 Prime Minister John Howard announced that a constitutional convention would be held 2–15 February 1999. The convention's purpose was to provide a forum for discussion about whether or not the constitution should be changed to permit the change to a republic. If so, which republic model should be put to the electorate to consider against the status quo? Finally, in what time frame and under what circumstances might any change be implemented?

To consider these weighty matters, a forum of 152 delegates was established, with half of that number being elected by the voting public and the other half appointed by invitation of the federal government. Of the 76 members appointed by the government, 40 were parliamentary representatives and the remaining 36 were non-parliamentary delegates. Almost inevitably at this stage, Trang was among the latter group as one of two delegates of Asian origin. National Party leader Ian Sinclair would chair the proceedings, with the ALP's Barry Jones as his deputy.

Trang, whose focus was on social policy issues and support for multiculturalism, had not given a great deal of thought to the appropriateness or otherwise of Australians swearing loyalty to a monarch on the other side of the world. It was an anachronism, certainly, but the Australian system of government was so deeply entrenched that she knew any change would be far more complex than simply shrugging off traditional loyalties and procedural inertia. Thus, while she was bemused when she was invited to participate in a convention to clarify the issues involved, she felt, as always, that her inclusion was both an honour and an opportunity to contribute that must not be missed.

Her fellow non-parliamentary delegates comprised a broad cross-section of high achievers from the churches, academia, Indigenous affairs, business, legal and community organisations. They included other noted academics including Professors Geoffrey Blainey, Greg Craven, Judith Sloan and George Winterton. Prominent female figures included Dr Lowitja (Lois) O'Donoghue, Dame Leonie Kramer, Dame Roma Mitchell and rising West Australian lawyer Julie Bishop, who in 2013 would become Minister for Foreign Affairs in the Abbott and Turnbull coalition governments. Trang already knew Ms Bishop quite well as a fellow member of the SBS Board. Clearly a great deal of thought had gone into the selection of a broad range of opinion, experience, conservatism and progressive thought. Trang looks back, almost in awe, to the experience of meeting and exchanging views with her fellow appointees:

> It was really an incredible experience. It seemed sometimes as if everybody who was anybody in Australia then was there. The republican side was headed by Malcolm Turnbull, later to become prime minister, who put a lot of money and effort into the convention. We were split into groups to consider particular issues. Following their discussions, all groups had a few minutes to put their case on TV and David taped that when it was my turn to speak. I had an argument openly with Geoffrey Blainey there. We were talking about whether the president should be Australian-born to be eligible.

Given Trang's consistent stance that an Australian was an Australian, regardless of ethnicity or birthplace, it would have been surprising if she hadn't challenged Professor Blainey on this point. She argued for a republic in which all citizens, regardless of origins, would be treated as equals. That she did so in a forum gathered to discuss Australia's constitutional future as a nation speaks to her strong self-belief and confidence in her equality as an Australian citizen. Her views made it clear that she was not just a representative of immigrant groups that had helped to grow the nation after World War II, but also of her community at large. 'If you limit eligibility for the presidency to people born in Australia,' she argued fiercely, 'you immediately create two classes of citizens. That is just not acceptable.' She summarises her thoughts on the outcome of the discussions:

> What did come out of the convention was that everyone agreed Australia would become a republic one day, but what form of republic was not agreed. Not many people liked the American system. And would there be direct voting for the president and how would that sit with the Westminster system? And the other thing is that many people believe that our present system of government works well. Why abolish it if a majority is comfortable with it? It's just the idea of it, I think. Most people like the idea of Australia being a republic. It is the question of the political model that is so complex. A very popular idea then was why don't we just have a parliamentary election, with two-thirds of the vote needed to elect a figurehead president? But there are

issues with power. The American president is very powerful. He can commit the country to war. He is not a figurehead.

The referendum was duly held in 1999 and failed to change the status quo. Arguably, the failure of the various elements of the republican movement to put forward a united, coherent plan for change contributed to the 'No' vote. 'The whole issue has gone rather quiet now,' says Trang. 'We have so many other pressing issues.'

Professor Trang Thomas, AM, 1997 Australia Day Honours List.

- CHAPTER 32 -

Return to Academia

Mumbai, January 2015

Trang was very much enjoying the company of friends in Mumbai, the gateway to India from the west. The sprawling giant, built across seven islands, developed over the centuries of Portuguese and British influence to become a present-day metropolis: the hub of the nation's largest financial, industrial and commercial enterprises, a booming IT industry and the make-believe world of Bollywood movies.

Shopping and sightseeing in the teeming city demand patience. However, the tour group's choice of centrally located accommodation, the Fariyas Hotel in Colaba, is within walking distance of many attractions. And when the day is done, there is time for Trang's biographer to delve further into her crowded past.

'Let's talk about the period leading to the turn of the century. You were resuming your job as Professor Trang at RMIT University at a time when your achievements outside academia were attracting growing recognition. Did you expect that your new emphasis on roles in psychology would bring a corresponding decrease in requests for your participation in national and multicultural affairs?'

Trang thinks back to those overcrowded years. 'There was still a lot on my plate, so much that I didn't give much thought to the longer term. I simply focused on meeting my immediate obligations. I suppose that, initially at least, I expected to have a lower profile once I'd worked through my existing appointments and settled back into the research fold. But that didn't happen. Instead, I continued to receive awards for my past efforts and I think that helped me to stay in contention for new opportunities.'

Melbourne, 1997–98

To Trang's surprise, her departure from the VMC had been marked by the 1997 Victoria Police Award in recognition of her contribution to community harmony. She was touched by the unexpected praise for what she regarded as one of many aspects of her job:

> My award was for liaison between the police and different immigrant groups. Some of the ethnic communities didn't have a very good relationship with the authorities. In their home countries, police were all too often associated with violence and corruption. Understandably, when they migrated to Australia they didn't have the same attitudes towards police and confidence in them as did the people of their new country. So the police established programs that promoted goodwill between the ethnic groups and themselves. I was able to facilitate access and help explain to the immigrants that they had come here into a different situation.

Having made the choice between the VMC and academia, Trang felt that the way ahead was clear. She would be engrossed in her duties both at the university and in the community roles she had already undertaken. And she knew that the requests for her participation were unlikely to cease. She had too many runs on the board. So many, in fact, that some observers might question whether her political leanings were a contributing factor in her appointments.

Typically, the question of merit versus favour is not an issue for Trang. She is proud of her record, which stems from appointments made by both sides of politics. However, she still feels that there were elements of 'right place, right time' and 'ticking the ethnic, female and academic boxes' in being approached to serve so often. Perhaps she is right. What really matters is that, whatever the combination of circumstances and talents that brought appointments her way, she justified her selection through her performance of the assigned tasks.

Even as she settled back into her academic career with renewed enthusiasm, requests she just could not turn down kept coming her way. Fortunately, RMIT University remained very supportive of her high-level involvement in public affairs. She was a double bonus for the institution, a high-profile academic whose reputation spilled over into its own and whose undiminished ability to attract research grants made her contribution to funding extremely valuable. The unprecedented decision seven years earlier to promote her directly from senior lecturer to a foundation chair had been justified in spades. And her employers were not alone in appreciating her talents and achievements. She had completed her PhD at La Trobe and her rapid progress since graduation had been noted there. To her surprise, in 1998 she was awarded La Trobe's inaugural Distinguished Alumni Award.

Once again, Trang was quite unprepared for the distinction bestowed upon her. The award was an acknowledgement that there had been many building blocks in her career since she had taken that first step into public affairs with her appointment as the ethnic affairs chair. Her life was like a pyramid under construction. Now there was yet another award to attract media attention and add to her standing in the community. She felt quite overwhelmed because it was an inaugural award, a great honour for any alumnus. There have been many very distinguished recipients since, so to be first among those names remains a great source of pride.

The award was presented by the Victorian Minister for Tertiary Education, Philip Honeywood. In response, Trang recalled her years at La Trobe as a life-changing experience that gave her confidence in the ability of women to achieve highly. It set her on the field of research that she had decided mattered most to her and in which she became a true leader. She also took the opportunity to make a strong statement of her belief that attitudes to multiculturalism and special assistance to disadvantaged groups in general should not be unduly influenced by those who regarded Australia's social and cultural broadening as an attack on their entrenched comfort zones:

> Multiculturalism is clearly undergoing a transformation. The challenge for us now is finding a clear vision of how we should live together in Australia and how to maintain respect for each other. The first step in the process may be acknowledging our shared values, our love of freedom and democracy and our unique respect for individual endeavour exemplified in the classic phrase 'a fair go for all'. These values are important and should be guarded. We should reject bigotry

and simple-minded appeals to the lowest common denominator, especially the selfish side of human nature, which has no place in a civilised society.

Her speech was widely reported and praised in the press and on SBS television, a fitting tribute to her popularity and status after years of service to the cause of multiculturalism.

Awards and publicity aside, Trang continued her frenetic pace throughout 1997-98. Her family progressed with her. She took great pride in David's continuing achievements and her daughters' progress in education. In 1998, she and David moved into their dream home at Yarra Bank Court, a two-storey dwelling overlooking the river. David would have preferred the sea, but the location was just right for their busy working lives. Now past fifty, Trang looked to the future with great anticipation. She didn't have long to wait before she was once more caught up in a new tide of events.

La Trobe University Chancellor Dr Sylvia Walton, presents Trang with La Trobe's inaugural Distinguished Alumni Award, 1997.

CHAPTER 32 - *Return to Academia*

Trang with fellow appointees to the Council for the Centenary of Federation, 1997-2001. Fellow appointees were Dick Smith (Chairman), Peter Hollingsworth, Angry Anderson, Betty Churcher, Evonne Goolagong and Rodney Cavalier.

- CHAPTER 33 -

Feminism and Recognition

Melbourne, 1999-2000

The fiftieth anniversary of the Australian Citizenship Act 1948 was celebrated in a book by eminent Australian, Wendy McCarthy AO. Her work, *A Fair Go: Portraits of the Australian Dream* (Focus Publishing, 1999), featured comprehensive profiles of fifty inspiring Australians who had begun their lives in another country and now served their adopted home in diverse fields with great distinction. Trang was chosen as one of the fifty, together with such stellar performers as Sir Arvi Parbo, Caroline Baum, Sarina Russo, Justice Jim Spigelman and Sir James Gobbo. Perhaps more than any honour or award she had received thus far, her inclusion in *A Fair Go* acknowledged her strong contribution to multiculturalism. 'I hope Australians of various heritages will treasure and maintain their culture in Australia but also feel detached enough to view actions of their countries of origin with dispassionate eyes,' she responded.

Trang's inclusion in *A Fair Go*, together with other female high achievers, also reflected the inroads made on discrimination against women during the second half of the twentieth century. The inexorable move towards gender equality as the norm, rather than a legislated set of rules for grudging compliance, brought new levels of acceptance. While equality remains a work in progress, women have since reached the very top political, business, academic and community appointments in twenty-first-century Australia. Trang is arguably one such beneficiary of changing attitudes and practices. Her history, as described thus far, begs the question of whether she is a strong but comparatively low-profile force for feminism or simply a high achiever who had the good fortune to adopt Australia as her home at the very time that determined feminists were breaking down long-established barriers.

The former view is supported by both Trang's own description of the events that shaped her career and comments provided by friends and family. Perhaps she is best described as a feminist by instinct. It is clear that, throughout her studies and subsequent career, negative experiences always fuelled her determination to make equality the norm.

Trang's quiet yet firm way of dealing with both workplace and social issues is perhaps the key reason why she has a lower public profile than prominent activists. Instead, her reputation as a strong defender of women's rights rests on a broader base of high-level academic and community service and her propensity to break through glass ceilings. It is difficult to be a strong voice without commensurate influence. Once having achieved a strong position alongside males, she did not hesitate to challenge them whenever they neglected to include her in their deliberations. She was also quick to reject traditional male attitudes to women in a number of ethnic communities during her time with the VMC. In this light, it can fairly be said that she has been a leader on the job rather than through emphasis on public advocacy.

Trang's ability to break new ground is publicly acknowledged by her inclusion in the National Pioneer Women's Hall of Fame, fittingly located in the very centre of Australia at Alice Springs. Founded in 1993, the Hall of Fame was moved to perhaps a more symbolic location, the Old Alice Springs Gaol, in 2007. That the institution was founded at all is a tribute to the impact of feminist thought. And that Trang should be included in its exhibition of high achievers and 'first timers' is a further tribute to changing attitudes and the growing acceptance of multiculturalism as genuine progress towards a more accommodating society.

The exhibition's theme includes the words 'Australian History Is Her Story Too'. In late 1999, Trang visited Alice Springs to see the Hall of Fame and her place in it. She felt deeply honoured by her inclusion. 'It is the kind of place that many tourists visit,' she says. 'Many people have called me to express surprise at finding a display about my life there.'

Coincidentally, and of great importance to women, 1999 also marked the passing into law of the Commonwealth Equal Opportunity in the

Workplace Act. The new legislation replaced the Commonwealth Affirmative Action Act of 1986. Thirteen years had passed since the affirmative action drive had really begun. Asked to comment on the progress made, Trang was positive:

> I just think that now, without the women's movement and effective legislation, discrimination would still be much more of a problem. People still wouldn't be aware of the need for women's participation at senior levels as well as lower down the scale. As we've discussed, as one of a relatively small cohort of female professors I was borrowed by metropolitan and regional Victorian universities to take part in many job interviews because it was mandatory to have persons of both genders on selection panels. It became difficult for me to meet the demand and I was very glad when more women became professors. There are now many women in the top ranks of academia, and the current generation of students and lecturers doesn't think it is a big deal. But it was a very big deal when I became the first female professor at RMIT.

Fittingly, 1999 closed with more family achievement. Elizabeth graduated in medicine from the University of Melbourne. That in turn led to another major event for Trang and David - their first child's marriage, on 12 February 2000. It was not just the start of a new phase of Elizabeth's life. 'It was quite an event because she married into a family with a Greek background,' Trang recalls fondly. 'Of course, she and her husband were both born in Australia so they are just Australian young people.' Elizabeth's husband, Dean Spilias, also shared her choice of profession. He was a graduate in medicine embarking on a career as a surgeon, while Elizabeth went on to specialise as a paediatrician. Her parents-in-law, Thanasis and Marian Spilias, high achievers themselves, are very proud of their eldest son and his family.

At the wedding, there were three cultures to celebrate: Greek, Vietnamese and Australian. It was hard to get a band that could play three types of music, but there was a family friend who sang in Vietnamese and, in accordance with tradition, there was much Greek music and dancing. But, like other young Australians, the younger family and guests just wanted contemporary music. 'They wanted to dance to that,' says Trang, 'so it was difficult to cater for everybody.'

Unfortunately, 2000 was to bring loss as well as joy. David's father passed away in August. To everyone's surprise, Arthur had outlived Sadie. His strong and supportive wife had fallen victim to lung cancer some years earlier. He had been very dependent on her, and, ever a relatively isolated man by choice, had elected after her passing to live on his own in a hostel. That did not sit well with his family, but it was the way he wanted it to be. True to his nature, he died as unobtrusively as he had lived.

Just months after her paternal grandfather's passing, second daughter Helen completed her studies in arts–commerce at the University of Melbourne with an honours year in history. She followed up with a Graduate Diploma in Editing and Publishing at RMIT University and commenced a successful career in that field. Helen is also well known as a soprano in Victorian opera and for her roles in musical and drama theatre. Trang was very proud of her appearances. 'In musicals her biggest role was as Mabel in *The Pirates of Penzance*. And she was Cosette in *Les Miserables*. At times like that I rounded up all of my students and supporters to cheer her on the opening night.'

As 2001 loomed, it seemed that Trang's future was mapped out for her. There was her position at RMIT. Her long engagement in planning for the centenary of Federation was almost complete. Her daughters were well educated and could look forward to fulfilling careers. David was contemplating a career change that would see him move from economics to law. She smiled fondly at him as fireworks announced the New Year and a new century. Maybe it would be a less demanding year, she told herself. Life was good and the next decade would see her with much more time to follow her own professional and family inclinations. She should have known better than to count her chickens so early in the decade, or in fact at all.

CHAPTER 33 - Feminism and Recognition

Trang visits her exhibit at the Pioneer Women's Hall of Fame, Alice Springs, 1999.

Elizabeth graduates in Medicine, University of Melbourne, 2000.

*Medical couple. Elizabeth marries Dean Spilias, Melbourne, 2000.
Dean is now a surgeon, Elizabeth a paediatrician.*

- CHAPTER 34 -

New Century, New Challenges

Goa, January 2015

'Are you familiar with the soaring music of Nikolai Rimsky-Korsakov's *Song of India*? I read somewhere that he was inspired by the unique, timeless strands of this country's civilisation, the grandeur that still overshadows the underlying struggle by its millions of poor to survive and prosper. Do you feel that timelessness?'

'I think I do,' Trang responded. 'I have travelled to many countries, but for me this place reflects in so many ways the sheer diversity of its ancestry and its cultural, religious and colonial influences. I feel its past so strongly even in its huge, modernising cities, like Mumbai. Just think of our experiences during the past three weeks. We've made our way from Delhi to Goa via Agra, Jaipur, Pushkar, Udaipur and Mumbai. It's like being in a different era, and often a different culture, every day. Like Goa's history of Portuguese colonisation that we've just explored. And I think our journey through the desert backblocks of Rajasthan might just have provided that glimpse of grandeur you mentioned. Is that where Rimsky-Korsakov travelled?'

'I have no idea. But now having seen the country, I like to think so. It certainly brought to mind so much of what I've read about the history of the subcontinent.'

Trang laughed. 'You love your history, don't you?'

'I do. Speaking of which, can you tell me more about your life after the turn of the century? Surely you couldn't have kept up the same pace for much longer?'

Melbourne, 2001-04

For a while it seemed that Trang's prediction of a quieter 2001 would come true. She had her professorial role and her appointments to the Casino and Gaming Authority and the SBS Board, but these were manageable. Her thoughts were now turning to what she might contribute to her professional body, the Australian Psychological Society (APS). Then she received the call. Federal Minister for Health Michael Wooldridge was offering her a position on the National Health and Medical Research Council (NHMRC). To refuse would have been contrary to all of her instincts and professional aspirations. She recalls her thoughts and experiences:

> It was both a great opportunity and a challenge, because it was a true medical research council. Most of the appointees were medicos and scientists in the biological and medical fields but it was very rare for a psychologist to be appointed. So a challenging aspect of my appointment was whether and to what extent my fellow councillors would appreciate the added diversity of knowledge and skills that I could contribute. Some might feel that health and medical research was rightly the preserve of medical research specialists. In the event, there was little overt questioning or resentment of my appointment. I had quite a happy time there. Certainly I've had worse. My colleagues were senior researchers, most of them professors. It is different when you are working with scientists. I didn't feel inferior in any way, and because of that it was okay. I stayed for two three-year terms, right through until 2007.
>
> The Council met for its deliberations on a monthly basis. Our primary functions were to advise the federal government on various health policies while administering a large health research grants scheme. There were unexpected issues as well. I was there during the 'mad cow disease' crisis. The problem originated in England but was international in its effects. I was a member of the expert committee appointed to determine how Australia would cope with the crisis, most importantly by learning more about the outbreak of the disease and assessing risk factors to compile a list of countries from which Australia could most

safely import beef. The Council also undertook contingency planning for responses to an outbreak of the disease in Australia, including early analysis of suspected casualties to confirm cause of death. I found it a scary but interesting experience.

Some tasks were easier than others, for example, when expert committees had already looked at grant applications for different fields of research. As the decision-making group at the top, councillors weren't involved at that preparatory level. However, my own experience as an applicant for research funding led me to take particular interest in the assessment processes. So I undertook a quality control exercise. I would listen to panel discussions and take notes, and if I found obvious flaws or questionable attitudes I would write that in my report.

One aspect that greatly disturbed Trang was the organisation's disregard for psychology. While looking at the responsibilities of various panels, she found applications for research grants in the field of child psychology being assessed by the group responsible for applications from paediatricians. She recalls being upset to find an application from a psychologist she knew, working in the area of developmental psychology, being assessed by medical specialists.

They had no idea about psychological research methods and didn't even think that the research was worthwhile. That explained why our profession had so little success with the Council in those days. Psychology didn't even have its own assessment panel. So I worked very hard trying to get psychologists accepted on those assessing panels, even just one or two to educate other members in the issues involved.

Another issue was that the NHMRC put little money into public health research grants. So I was running around trying to get people to pay more attention to grants in that area, especially mental health issues. I was absolutely upset by how little regard was paid to psychology in such an important area. So I requested that special funding be allocated to research into public health issues instead of just into specific biological and medical areas. And, once the decision was made to allocate a certain percentage of the budget into public health, then applications began to arrive. I recall that Professor Fiona Stanley, a leader in child and public health research, received quite a large sum for research into children's health. So I was very proud to be able to contribute to reforms in the culture of the organisation during my two terms.

Trang's appointment to the Council was thus more than a new feather in her cap. Her determined approach to her duties confirmed her professionalism and commitment to reform. In turn, recognition of her achievements opened new doors. In this case, the rare distinction of being a member of the NHMRC promoted her standing in the APS. She was encouraged to stand for election to the APS Board and was successful.

Once again, her plate was more than full. But 2001 was not over, and it was soon after her election as an APS director that she received the call yet again. The UN had scheduled a conference on racism in Durban, South Africa, for early November. The Australian delegation, set up by the Howard government, was led by Senator Kay Patterson. Trang was one of three delegates chosen to represent ethnic communities. She tells an interesting and eye-opening story of her experience:

> The conference was held just before the 9/11 terrorist attacks in the United States. There were twenty-three heads of state there. I met Fidel Castro for example. An amazing presence, but of course I couldn't understand what he said. But the way he looked and talked was so charismatic. And Yasser Arafat was there. To meet these international figures was a quite different and memorable experience for me. Unfortunately, however, there were no ground-breaking outcomes. It just gave everybody a chance to talk, a forum to air their grievances. Nothing new, but there were various groups who had been treated badly, like the gypsies, the Roma people. They talked about how they were persecuted around the world.
>
> Almost inevitably, the proceedings became a forum for national grievances as well. There was a lot of anti-American and anti-Israel sentiment, to the point where the Israeli and American groups withdrew. That made matters worse. I don't think any of the talking achieved much. So we came home and one week later 9/11 happened. Can you imagine the chaos if the terrorist attacks had taken place while we were

in Durban? How would you protect so many heads of state?

For Trang, the conference also brought a personal experience that has stayed with her. Until Durban, she had never thought of herself as being what South Africans referred to as 'coloured'. In Australia she'd been treated without bias for so long that she always thought of herself as just Trang Thomas rather than a white or yellow or black Trang Thomas. But at that conference, the location ensured that skin colour was a big deal. Her awakening came when she ventured out into the community:

> In Durban, because we were officials from other countries, we were very well protected. The Australian Embassy hired five drivers, bodyguards really, who were always there to look after us. I wasn't even allowed to cross the street on my own. So whenever I wanted to go somewhere I'd have to call this mobile number and one of those five guys would come to accompany me. There was one that I came to regard as my bodyguard. He was so nice and on one occasion he took me for a drive to various areas in Durban where people just came out on to the street and stared at me. 'You would not last five minutes,' he told me, 'if you were out of the car or had to drive through this area by yourself. You are okay because you are with me.' And then another time, I asked him: 'It seems there is a white people's group and a black people's group. And that you belong to the black group. Is that right?' He was quite offended. 'I'm coloured,' he said, 'not black!' I was so ignorant that I just had no idea that people were so sensitive about colour. And all the time I was there little things reminded me that I am not white. Not black either, but the topic was always out there. On television there was constant reference to black and white. Never since I came from Vietnam to live in Australia had anyone looked at me and said: 'You are not white.' So that's the experience I took away from Durban, a week of constant reminders that I am not white. And of course we went to the Apartheid Museum. One of the items was a bench that was marked 'White Only'. It was awful, an experience that drove home the realisation that skin colour was such a major determinant of status in certain societies.

Proving once more that her life has had no really dull moments, Trang capped a frenetic 2001 with a new appointment that would engage her for the next two years. The announcement came that, during 2002–04, the Australian Human Rights Commission (AHRC) would conduct an inquiry into the controversial issue of refugee children being held in detention by the Australian immigration authorities. Trang was named as one of two Assistant Human Rights Commissioners who would assist the Commissioner, Dr Sev Ozdowski, to conduct the inquiry.

'You've done it again,' said David. 'It had to happen, of course. It would be unthinkable for you to have any fewer than five or six jobs at a time. Thank God I've learned to cook.'

Trang at the United Nations Conference on Racism, Durban, South Africa, November 2001.

- CHAPTER 35 -

Human Rights and Refugee Children

Canberra, 2002-04

When the Inquiry into Refugee Children in Detention Centres was announced by the AHRC in 2001, the issue of children (defined as under eighteen) being held in detention with their parents was not new. It was almost a decade since the Keating Labor government had responded to an influx of refugees by introducing mandatory detention for all asylum seekers.

It was a complex and challenging issue, not least since many family groups, beset by anxiety and mistrust of the authorities, would find it difficult to cope with separation if the children were housed elsewhere. A strong debate developed between those who supported the government's policy and those who opposed detention of asylum seekers on principle as an abrogation of Australia's responsibilities as a signatory to the United Nations Convention on Refugees. It was this debate that led to the AHRC's inquiry.

Human Rights Commissioner Dr Sev Ozdowski and Trang were joined by Assistant Commissioner Dr Robin Sullivan (Commissioner for Children and Young People, Queensland). Dr Sullivan came from a distinguished career in education, having become Queensland's first female Director-General of Education in 1997.

Dr Ozdowski was no stranger to Trang. During her years as Ethnic Affairs Commissioner in Victoria, Ozdowski had been her counterpart in South Australia. They shared many values, including a strong commitment to Australia and what it meant to be an Australian citizen. Both had become well known for their representation of ethnic communities and support for equal rights in a multicultural Australia. And both had migrated from countries identified with severe violations of human rights, the source of many refugees who had eventually found new homes in Western democracies. Finally, both had strong records of integrity and objectivity in their academic and representative careers. When the inquiry got under way, these strengths were reflected in the comprehensive and consultative way in which it was conducted.

Trang has strong memories of her experience, especially the searing images of despair and protest in some of the refugee centres:

> I went out into the field myself, visiting each detention centre and actually meeting many of the asylum seekers. So there was lots of travelling. We would stay in motels and during the days we would go into the centres to talk to the asylum seekers to collect our data. We also had some staff, so there was a team of us. The one centre I didn't visit was on the island of Nauru. The other commissioners went, but I had to miss that trip. It might have been a little better there. The detainees were allowed to swim at the beaches, so at least the atmosphere might be a little brighter.
>
> Having said that, when you see such places it is really hard to believe that this is Australia. But as always there were two sides to the story. When we went inside the centres, many of the detainees were very stubborn. They made demands we knew the Australian government would not meet. Nevertheless I still wished such places didn't exist here. The barbed wire, the narrow access lanes, locked compounds, the need to protect single women, the innocent children. The detainees played football with the guards to learn English. But the next day they could riot and throw rocks at the guards they'd been interacting with so constructively the day before.
>
> I recall in particular the notorious Woomera Centre. It was a much more harrowing experience than the others because a major protest by the detainees was in progress when we visited. There was a riot, with some of the asylum seekers sewing their lips together and others occupying the rooftops. The guards sprayed water to get them to come

down. I walked along those narrow lanes lined on both sides with barbed wire, with people behind the wire on both sides. Some had their lips sewn together and others screamed abuse at us because they thought we were officials from the government. I wasn't scared so much as upset that such a thing could be happening on Australian soil. For the first time since my arrival in 1964 I felt ashamed to call myself an Australian. And one of the very sad aspects was that many of the asylum seekers would have been ideal immigrants under other circumstances. I met this family from Iran whose father had been a university professor there. There were three children, including two teenage girls, who were very intelligent. They said they were doing very well at school, and then one day their father told them to pack because they were leaving. They went to various camps and ended up in the detention centre. They were so depressed, so damaged. Eventually the family was permitted to stay on humanitarian grounds. It was sad because the family had so much to contribute to this country and we had put them into detention centres and damaged them thoroughly and then we let them stay anyway. It was a very complex issue for all and still is, and I really don't know how all of the problems can be solved. There are just no easy solutions for either side.

There was much more to the commissioners' work than travelling to visit detention centres. Evidence was also gathered from meetings with a wide range of groups and individuals including refugee advocates, healthcare professionals and the responsible government department (Immigration, Multicultural and Indigenous Affairs). Their work completed, the commissioners' findings were published in a damning report entitled *National Inquiry into Children in Immigration Detention Report - A Last Resort?* The report found that the detention policy had led to many instances of breaches of human rights and had not complied with Australia's obligations as a signatory to the UN Convention on the Rights of the Child. In particular, it had failed to make the detention of children a measure of 'last resort' subject to independent review.

The report sparked a nationwide debate, leading to a review by the Howard government of refugee detention policies. Significant reforms ensued, including the release of children and their mothers from detention to other accommodation in local communities.

The sadness of the children was the enduring impression that Trang took with her and retains today. The debate concerning Australia's treatment of asylum seekers continues, now in the context of refugee numbers as a global issue. 'It is such a multifaceted problem,' she says, 'not just for Australia but now for the whole world. The barriers to its resolution are enormous.'

Career change. David graduates as Doctor of Jurisprudence, Melbourne, 2003.

- CHAPTER 36 -

Director of Science, Australian Psychological Society

Melbourne, 2004

The completion of the Inquiry into Children in Detention was welcome in the sense that it enabled Trang to give more time to her responsibilities as a director of the APS. Australia's largest non-medical professional health body, the society had steadily grown since the mid-twentieth century to represent more than 22,000 registered psychologists by 2015. The Board is responsible for governance of the society, advocacy for its members, oversight of existing programs and strategic planning for continuing effectiveness of professional education and development. That is no small task.

Trang's first hurdle was the division of responsibilities among the directors. Membership, practitioner standards, science and research, community issues and other matters are allocated to individual directors for oversight. The community issues position had traditionally been filled by a woman, and when she was elected she was expected to take it. But she has always resisted stereotyping and was not prepared to be told what position a female should undertake. Her position on the NHMRC added to her confidence in her academic research record. So she instead put herself forward for appointment to the science position, which had traditionally been filled by a high-profile male. She made a strong case and succeeded.

Given her strong views, Trang's decade of experience as an APS director was not a bed of roses. In the beginning, she found it difficult to operate within a strongly male culture. She smiles at the memories:

> It sometimes involved lots of drinking. We often had restaurant meals together, a kind of bonding exercise, and I felt quite shocked about the amount of alcohol consumed and the expense involved. It was the

members' money, after all. But as time went on the culture changed, in particular after we started electing female presidents. When Amanda Gordon was president, she said: 'When we go out to dinner, do not order expensive wine that you would not usually order if you were going out for other occasions.' Amanda was quite a strong president. She brought in a lot of changes.

Trang remained the APS Director for Science for two terms, and is proud to say that gender is no longer particularly relevant to board duties. There is now nothing unusual about having a female science director or indeed a female president. Having said that, she cautions against the assumption that the APS is now run by women and men in roughly equal proportions. The current ratio of female to male membership is approximately 7:3. Yet the majority of presidents are still men. Honorary Fellowships go overwhelmingly to men, with only one female recipient at present. Most professors are still men. 'So even given that more women are coming to the fore,' she insists, 'the men are still running the show.'

Why is it so? Trang has given much thought to gender-based roles and family circumstances:

> I believe that men are more focused on their careers. Almost inevitably, women's careers are less stable. Most drop out of the workforce from time to time to bear and nurture children or for other family reasons, such as caring for elders. Some manage to work part time to stay in touch and earn a living. That is a sound strategy for the longer term, but the cost of childcare is prohibitive. Lengthy distractions and work limitations obviously affect experience and progress, whether academically or as a practitioner. But there is arguably another factor that holds women back. I believe that many don't put themselves forward as assertively as men. So sometimes they accept second best for no good reason. It is the same in universities, in corporations everywhere. A lot of women just don't push hard enough to fulfil their potential. As an example from my own experience, in my honours year at UNSW, five students, all girls, achieved first-class honours. Of those five, I am the only one who went on to become a professor. Others raised families, going back only after the children had grown up. Or they had big gaps in their careers

for other reasons. Conversely, those students who gained Honours 2A or 2B, many of them males, went on to achieve more highly. More often than not they did so with the support and commitment of their female partners.

For those women who wish for both family and success in their field, patience and commitment are essential. I have given many motivational talks to girls and young women. I always tell them that there is no need to be greedy, to have it all straight away, that there is a time to have their children and their home and there is then time to aim higher in their profession again. The fact is that, at any given point, you have to make that choice about what is best for you. About what you want most. Take my own experience. I took time off my studies and focus on career to raise my kids and only returned to undertake my PhD when they had grown to school age and I could take that time. And I was lucky that, when I did go back to focus on qualifications and career opportunities, my career blossomed.

To put it another way, I don't believe that you should abandon your career because the kids are too important. On the other hand, I don't believe you should regard your career as too important to have your kids. It is possible to do both, just not at the same time. If you are committed and assertive, you will get on. The key to building success after a long absence is to work very hard to improve your expertise and to make the strongest possible case for your advancement whenever an opportunity comes.

Reflecting on her first four years as Director of Science following her election in 2001, Trang points out that she was prepared to make her mark by breaking further new ground. When she was elected, a Manager of Science and Education was appointed as well. The selection process brought Dr Mary Katsikitis, an experienced clinical psychologist from the Department of Psychiatry at Adelaide University, to the new position. Dr Katsikitis was responsible for managing accreditation and professional development processes for APS members. She and Trang set the ball rolling by travelling together throughout Australia, talking to the heads of departments to promote the scientific aspects of psychology. Trang recalls the experience with pride:

> We encouraged strongly a focus on research aspects as well as the clinical teaching. We looked at the courses available for training of postgraduate students and encouraged a more scientific approach where that seemed necessary. It was unusual, of course, to have two women going around together on that sort of exercise. But it worked well. Mary, now a professor at the University of the Sunshine Coast, is very dynamic and assertive, not at all hesitant about putting forward a strong case for reform to heads of departments. We had a very good time working together, and were responsible for a lot of initiatives and changes.

For both Trang and Mary, that was the start of a long and productive relationship. In an appointment related to her position as Director of Science, Trang later served as a director of the Australian Psychology Accreditation Council (APAC) from 2007 to 2009. The task was to visit universities as required to evaluate and provide accreditation for new schools and their courses. Trang speaks very highly of Mary's role:

> It wasn't my primary task, of course, just another of my many responsibilities. As the Manager for Science and Education, Mary took the initiative. Her thoughts and ideas were the basis for our activities. She remains very much involved with the accreditation process to this day, still a member of APAC and holding other positions, including National Course Approvals Chair for the APS College of Clinical Psychologists and membership of the APS Program Development and Accreditation Committee.

Taking on different roles and looking for new possibilities for enhancement of professional standards was the norm during Trang's decade as an APS director. One such initiative was inspired by her aim to foster cross-cultural awareness among members and to facilitate their involvement with overseas colleagues to gain a broader understanding of the challenges involved in treating mental illnesses in diverse cultural settings. She was very much aware that Australian practitioners operated in an increasingly multicultural society in which immigration flows include traumatised asylum seekers from many source countries, as well as aged people with fixed attitudes and beliefs. In therapeutic approaches, one size does not fit all, or even most. It was time, she concluded, to put in place a regular contribution to professional development through visits by practitioners to other countries.

Trang draws on her experience as Assistant Human Rights Commissioner to address APS colleagues on immigrant detention issues in the mid-2000s.

- CHAPTER 37 -

Driving Cross-cultural Initiatives

Melbourne, 2004-11

Trang acknowledges that her idea of a professional development program combined with travel was scorned by some of her colleagues. The conservative APS leadership followed the established professional norm of promoting Australian research and practice through participation in international conferences. In their view, that was the most effective way of establishing contacts and sharing common aspirations. That was how you met colleagues from overseas, not by mixing business with tourism. It was hinted that Trang might more suitably make the switch from psychologist to travel agent.

Undaunted by criticism, Trang persevered and her efforts to address cultural issues in psychological treatment were tolerated. Her cross-cultural initiative was in fact not a new idea. It was in large part founded in her four years of experience as Victoria's Ethnic Affairs Commissioner during the 1990s. At that time, her frequent meetings with community leaders highlighted, among many other issues, the difficulties inherent in providing mental health services across linguistic and cultural boundaries. So she had long been conscious of the problem, and now that she was in a position to address the issue her thoughts had turned to what might be done to raise awareness among her peers and to forge links with like-minded professionals in other countries.

Among the community leaders she met frequently during her time as the ethnic affairs chief was Stephen Seif, a leader of the Coptic Egyptian Community. Stephen organised tours taking mainly second-generation immigrants back to Egypt for them to learn more about their heritage. In

1996 he invited Trang to accompany him as part of a group that included politicians from both major parties. The group attracted considerable attention in Egypt, including a reception arranged by the Minister for Culture. 'That's how it all began,' says Trang. 'I enjoyed the experience and revisited the country with friends. At that time I wasn't really thinking as much about professional development as cultural awareness. And then on one of the trips I decided we should visit the university in Cairo. I met the professor of psychology there and invited him to visit Australia.'

The APS sponsored the Egyptian professor's visit from funds set aside for the provision of psychological services in developing countries. The Society funded one visit a year, giving time for each visitor to learn much about the practice of psychology in Australia. The visits were of great value to practitioners who sought to advance the profession in their own countries as well as establishing enduring professional links. Trang's initiative in Egypt was the beginning of a regular program of visits by APS psychologists to countries worldwide. Her initial thought was to examine attitudes and approaches to psychological practice in countries with very old and strong cultures, in which psychology was a relatively recent concept as a treatment for mental health issues. In Egypt, she found that, even at the university where psychology was taught, it was at a very low level and facilities were poor. On subsequent visits to other Middle Eastern countries, including Syria and Jordan, she was unable to gain sufficient access to public facilities to be able to assess properly the level of mental health services. Her group did manage to visit a psychiatric hospital, a private facility in which treatment appeared to be of a fairly high standard. 'But private hospitals there are only for the wealthy,' she says. 'They had patients there who had come from other countries for treatment. We were not allowed to go into a public hospital so we didn't know what the treatment was like there.'

Since that tentative beginning, Trang and her colleagues have exposed many practising Australian psychologists to various country-specific cultural barriers to treatment and the ways in which problem issues were being addressed in those places. From its beginnings in the Middle East, the professional development tour program gradually extended to Europe, Asia and South America. Other tour leaders emerged, some of whom spoke the languages of prospective host countries. Trang feels that the program has been a success:

> It has been so popular with members. Many who joined the tour groups were women who wanted to visit overseas facilities but felt safer travelling in a group than on their own. They had to pay the costs involved either way. And it was better to go with a group because, for obvious reasons, it is much more difficult for one person to gain access to the facilities we visited. Soon there was a network of colleagues in Australia who were interested in cross-cultural development and networks grew in other countries as well. Of course tours were combined with other activities – sightseeing and travelling around the countries concerned. But, during the tours, we always exchanged a lot of ideas and knowledge. For example, while on tour each participant must attend regular professional development meetings and take their turn to make presentations on their own field of practice and how it fits into a multicultural setting. I think it is a real win-win activity.

Closer to home, Trang was surprised to discover that her views on ethnic minorities and their rights to equality could put her at odds with her colleagues in New Zealand.. In 2006, she was selected to chair an Australia-New Zealand Joint Conference. She recalls that it was a very interesting experience for her because of the attitudes she encountered:

> New Zealand has the Treaty of Waitangi, which specifies that it is a bicultural country. The white and Maori cultures are regarded as equal, and the rest don't matter. I bombarded them with questions about that, simply because they kept repeating that their country is bicultural. They were unfortunate that they encountered me, a person who insisted that, in any country with immigrant minorities, all ethnicities and cultures must be regarded as equal. 'No, no, no!' they insisted. 'The English and Maori cultures are equal. Don't worry about the rest.'

> I really gave them a hard time, and we did have a few fights because they said at the opening of the conference that their constitution mandated the acknowledgement of the Maori people and the English people. And I said: 'No. Every culture or none at all. Because we must respect multiculturalism.' After that they said it would be a long time before

they held another joint conference. I really felt quite upset about it, that they would insist their country was bicultural rather than multicultural.

Trang's clash with her New Zealand colleagues is a telling example of her determination to address indifference to multiculturalism and the question of equal rights for all citizens of a country, wherever she finds it. Fortunately, the disagreement did not result in lasting animosity. In 2007, she returned to New Zealand to attend another conference. 'They must have forgiven me,' she smiles wryly. 'They let me back in.'

Humour aside, and while it is easy to view Trang's often spectacular progress as one along a river riddled with sandbars that she navigated with aplomb, there were many other occasions when her assertive approach did not win through. She recalls the entrenched attitudes she so often encountered:

> My community appointments and interaction with ethnic communities could be quite stressful. On all of these boards and councils I was in a minority of females or even the only one. And very often I was the only ethnic person. The men tended to take over and run everything. So I had to speak up quite strongly sometimes, or I would just be ignored. And if there was something good coming up, the men would assume they'd be the ones to take it. I'd have to remind them that I too might be interested.

Inevitably, Trang put a lot of noses out of joint. She made enemies as well as friends. And they were not confined to the male-dominated institutions in which she would unexpectedly find herself occupying senior roles. Some of the board and committee positions she undertook were voluntary. So if she was refused a voice then she'd simply resign. That was particularly so on committees in the Vietnamese community. They were dominated by men, often ex-army officers. Such men were used to having their way, so it could be very difficult for a woman to be heard. The men wanted very much to maintain the old ideals from the Vietnamese culture. 'Second-generation males were different,' she recalls. 'They were not so political. Many had been born after the Vietnam War. But the elders were strongly traditional. That didn't suit me. I didn't want to cling on to the old hostilities. So if they went on about it I'd just walk away.'

- CHAPTER 38 -

Sailing before the Wind

Kasane, Botswana, August 2015

The late afternoon river cruise along Botswana's Chobe River, a tributary of the mighty Zambesi, takes the traveller through a world of colour and movement. The feast of birdlife is a twitcher's dream, from scavenging marabou storks to the blue flashes of tiny kingfishers nesting in the mudbanks. A large island midstream literally teems with elephant and hippo families flanked by large, watchful crocodiles and herds of surefooted red lechwe antelopes. The incomparable African sunset bathes the river and its surrounds in vivid light. Back at the Chobe Marina Lodge at Kasane, warthogs forage complacently in the mature garden settings of riverside accommodation. For Trang and her travel companions, this is the final highlight of a tour that began two weeks earlier in Cape Town.

As always, Trang finds the tour and the companionship relaxing. The last decade of her working and family life had brought both rewards and the chill of loss and grief. Tomorrow, after the morning game drive and lunch, she would relate the ups and downs of those years to her biographer. It was by now an established custom as much as a research exercise. Trang found it somehow easier in these relaxed, exotic surroundings to put her memories into perspective and let the words flow.

Melbourne: Work, family, travel, 2001-08

Trang was not alone in taking on new challenges. As the new century dawned, David had decided on a change of direction, a move motivated in part by a restructure of Swinburne University. He was already ambivalent about the prospect of continuing his economic research ad infinitum, so he elected to take a separation package and start a new career. Never one to take the easy road, from 2001 to 2003 he achieved his lifetime dream of becoming a lawyer by undertaking further postgraduate studies and duly graduating as a Doctor of Jurisprudence (JD).

Following his graduation, David applied for and was appointed to positions on both the Superannuation Complaints and Migration Review tribunals, where his background in economics and his new legal qualification fitted him well for the deliberations involved. He was able to serve concurrently on the two tribunals because neither was full time. Sitting fees were paid by the day. Trang recalls that he was very busy. The Superannuation Tribunal position was particularly demanding because both sides of politics kept changing the already-complex framework of rules. Keeping up with the legislation was a task in itself. The Migration Review Tribunal work was also complex, and it was here that he enjoyed the benefit of first-hand knowledge of cross-cultural and immigration issues through his exposure to Trang's work in these fields as well as his own extensive travels.

Notwithstanding its complications, David loved his work. His stable and satisfying employment situation was thus a rock in Trang's life, enabling her to continue her rise and rise during the mid-2000s. Trang reflects with pride on his career move:

> He enjoyed it so much. I eventually retired, but he worked on until illness eventually forced him to give it up. So he had more than ten years working as a lawyer. He still loved his politics, of course, and took every opportunity to assist people he believed in with their campaigns. He was really good in that role - the man behind the candidate. Helping people to succeed. He did not aspire to becoming a representative, because, despite his commitment, he realised that to become successful in politics one needed to have certain qualities that he didn't have, such as tolerance of ignorance. So he was very happy to have his second career in law.

Meanwhile, the years following the completion of the Inquiry into Children in Detention and Trang's election to the APS Board of Directors were notable also for her continuing research supervision at RMIT, her continuing role at the NHMRC and her perennial support for ethnic communities. She continued to emphasise the importance of multiculturalism and equal rights for women. The years were also marked by ongoing recognition of her record of service. The award of the Centenary Medal in 2003 highlighted yet again her enthusiastic embrace of Australia as her new home from the 1970s and her key roles in professional and community affairs. Then, in 2005, Trang's name was added to the Victorian Women's Honour Roll. On this occasion the honour was not a surprise because she had been forewarned. 'I knew something about it,' she says. 'Joan Kirner chaired a committee that discussed these matters and I was included among those whose name was to be added. Mary Delahunty was the Minister for Women, and when she gave it to me she said it was long overdue.'

Trang was pleased to be recognised by the Victorian sisterhood in this way. But there was more, much more to celebrate than personal achievement. Family was, as always, of paramount importance. On 15 November 2003, Helen married academic historian Sam Koehne. The Koehne family was of Germanic origin, and the wedding therefore added another dimension of multiculturalism to the extended family. Trang and David were experiencing the joy of a growing kinship group and looking forward eagerly to the milestone that they had long dreamed of, the arrival of their first grandchild. There was much to be thankful for as the decade rolled on, and more to come.

Trang looks upon the mid-2000s as a time when, although she was as productive as ever, she did not feel under as much pressure as in some of the earlier years. Instead, she recalls the period as a relative comfort zone because her children were married and had their own careers and family commitments. David, too, was settled into his tribunal roles and, in all, there was more time for them to share. In 2007, for example, they took advantage of Trang's APS commitments in New Zealand to tour the country together.

Truly an inveterate traveller, Trang was by this time a very experienced tour leader and tourist guide. 'These are the places you should not miss,' she would tell her charges. 'And if you want to shop I will show you where to go for the best quality and price.' In her rewarding but still overflowing life, the APS professional development tours were a saving grace. Despite their crowded itineraries, there was time to review her multiple tasks and reset her priorities. Whatever her commitments, she made time to visit new places. During 2003–08 she attended psychology conferences at popular travel destinations, including Rhodes, Ontario, Prato (Italy), Paris and New Zealand. In 2004 she led the first official APS tour to the Middle East. In the group was Dr Mary Katsikitis, her colleague and Manager of Science in the APS. The tours had continued, first to Turkey and then to Vietnam and Cambodia, becoming an established contribution to the professional development of many APS psychologists.

David was usually unable to accompany Trang due to his own commitments. However, he didn't mind being left alone. 'He actually enjoyed it,' says Trang. 'He was always quite happy with his own company for a week or two. Then I'd be back and it would seem almost as though I hadn't been away.'

Trang reflected often on her good fortune that doors continued to open for her, prompting her to wonder what she had done in her previous incarnations to deserve such a fulfilling life. For her, Australia really was the Lucky Country. As one who had made Australia her new home and had pursued a successful career over four decades, she was proud of the fact that post-World War II immigration had played such a significant role in the growth and development of the nation as a diverse cultural entity. The population had almost doubled during that time. She had just one major concern. The way forward for multiculturalism was increasingly difficult to predict. The political furore concerning the treatment of asylum seekers had abated with the implementation of the 'Pacific Solution' of offshore processing of asylum seekers' claims. Nevertheless, the flow of criticism from refugee advocates continued. In their view, Australia's obligations to any person who claimed refugee status outweighed any and all other considerations. The other side of the coin was the broader public's fear of the social and economic consequences of an 'open border' policy and the possible spread of terrorist attacks to Australia following 9/11, the Bali bombings and other atrocities. Trang hoped fervently that Australia would be spared the turmoil of multiple attacks that would feed the growing polarisation of attitudes to immigrants from troubled countries.

On the federal scene, in 2007 the Howard government was replaced by that of Labor leader Kevin Rudd. That change of power and the subsequent relaxation of border security led quickly to a resumption of the rapid increase in refugee boat arrivals. Given the effort that she had put into the earlier Inquiry into Children in Detention and her relief at the Howard government's moves to address its findings and recommendations, Trang could not help but be disheartened by the surge in human trafficking that followed the 2007 election and the implications for the number, inevitably including children, in detention facilities:

> I felt that this divisive situation would never end, and perhaps it won't. It is no longer an issue of open or closed borders or our responsibilities to ensure the observance of human rights and refugee conventions. It is much, much more complex than that because it involves so many political, economic and cultural factors other than those that prevailed when the UN established its conventions.

At this time, one of many interesting episodes in Trang's life was an extended visit in 2007 to Myanmar under the auspices of a UNICEF project. Myanmar was still boycotted by neighbouring countries and its defensive military government was hostile to outside interest in its affairs, even in the form of UN initiatives. Despite the difficulties involved, UNICEF had already established numerous programs helping women and children, in particular in the areas of children's nutrition, health and wellbeing. One aspect of growing concern was that there were many social problems within the country, but no professional social workers to help address them. A social work course was therefore set up at Yangon University to train local social workers using overseas professionals to provide a curriculum and conduct the training. Trang was asked to go there to teach the psychology content. 'It took a long time to get permission from the Myanmar government,' she recalls. 'And even when I finally got there in 2007 the government didn't cooperate to make things easier for UNICEF.'

Trang, who would spend several weeks teaching her part of the curriculum, was surprised to learn that Yangon University had a well-established Department of Psychology. However, its teaching materials were very outdated. Trang's answer was to take with her a large suitcase full of books and papers, especially the latest on clinical psychology. 'The staff were just so grateful that it was embarrassing,' she recalls. 'The books they were using were ten years out of date, teaching material that nobody in Australia would ever use.'

Fortunately, there were few communication problems because the teaching was in English. So Trang had no difficulty working with the faculty staff, some of whom had been trained overseas before this practice was forbidden. The students on the course were not as proficient as the staff, but were sufficiently advanced for Trang and her fellow lecturers to be able to teach them. It was another memorable experience, even more so because one of the professors spent a day driving her around to see places of interest in Yangon. She was told later that he had to queue for two hours to get the petrol. 'I just felt so bad,' she says wryly. 'It just showed how difficult even everyday life in a struggling country could be. And yet I know that he was happy to do something in return for my efforts to help. It certainly ensured that I have good memories of my time there.'

Professional matters aside, the real highlight of 2007 was the long-awaited first grandchild. David and Trang's dream was realised when little Evie was born to Elizabeth and Dean. 'I went out and spent lots of money on baby stuff,' Trang recalls fondly. 'No expense spared. It was very special because Elizabeth had tried before and miscarried. So it hadn't been an easy road to motherhood. When Evie came it was a time of joy for the whole family.' Joy came again the following year when their second granddaughter, Rebecca, was born to Helen and Sam. These special events heightened their pride in the achievements of their daughters. Well-educated professionals, they were now adding a new generation to the family. Ensconced in their dream home overlooking the Yarra, David and Trang gave thanks that so many of the threads of their lives had come together in a cloak of satisfying texture. Their professional lives remained fulfilling and they shared happily the routine duties of home and family. So much for the naysayers who had predicted their marriage would not last because of ethnic and cultural differences. It was a good feeling.

Despite the calmer waters she had reached, Trang, even as she continued to meet the demands placed on her by her own enthusiasm and capacity for work, knew that she couldn't maintain the pace forever. The years of commitment were beginning to take their toll, yet work remained a deeply entrenched part of her life, an activity she could not think of ceasing. Looking back, she sees the arrival of grandchildren Evie and Rebecca as the catalyst for a reallocation of her priorities. Being a grandparent brought a significant new dimension to life that must be enjoyed in full. After all, nothing was more important and fulfilling than participating in the exploratory steps of a new generation. There was much for her to consider as she set about reordering her work-life balance.

A special family occasion as Helen marries academic Sam Koehne, Melbourne, 2005.

Colleague Dr Mary Katsikitis and husband George, join Trang for her 60th birthday, Lyceum Club, Melbourne, 2006.

First grandchild. Evie is born to proud parents Dean and Elizabeth, 2007.

- CHAPTER 39 -

Retirement from RMIT University

Melbourne, 2008

In October 2008, Trang had to address an issue she had been trying to ignore. Now that she was in her sixties, the robust physical health that had served her so well was declining. For some time she had coped with a knee injury that finally required surgery. While the operation was moderately successful and she recovered a good deal of her mobility, she found it necessary to use a cane for work and travel. Then, during the following year, she also underwent cataract surgery and was diagnosed with diabetes. Typically, she decided she would not let these nuisance ailments prevent her from continuing her active life. She was determined to remain busily involved with work, family and community. But something had to go. Reluctantly, she decided to step away from her academic career.

Her contribution to RMIT's programs, from undergraduate students to post-doctoral research, had spanned almost three decades. During her seventeen years as a professor, her achievements both on and off campus had invariably reflected well on her university. Her long and eminent service was formally recognised by her appointment as Emeritus Professor. This honour means that she keeps her title for life. It also carries modest staff privileges, including access to the library and email facilities. In return, she was to provide unpaid assistance for projects that benefit from her expertise in research, including supervision and marking theses. 'RMIT has only fourteen emeritus professors,' she says with pride. 'And not a lot are women.'

Reflecting on this major change in her working life, Trang does not feel any great sense of sadness at retiring:

> I still have my office, and I still turn up about once a month. Some of the staff I worked with are still there. And I have my mailbox. But of course I get busier and busier with my own affairs and RMIT becomes a smaller part of my life. It is just a slow process, and a nice way to wind up an academic career. I think I retired at just the right time. I felt I'd done enough, and I was getting tired of chasing research grants.

Trang also reshaped her community interests. In 2008, she resigned from her appointment as a director of the Victorian Board of Alzheimer's Australia, a position she had accepted in 2003. Her interest in the organisation had flowed naturally from her research into health issues of ageing and her membership of the Australian Association of Gerontology. She was thus well known in those circles and had in fact been a keynote speaker at an Alzheimer's conference.

As a state body, the Victorian organisation was mainly involved in the provision of services to the families of Alzheimer's sufferers. She explains its role:

> Most of the research and funding is at the federal level. However, the state organisation provides very good support and advice to people on how to handle afflicted persons. One disappointing thing is that not enough people use the services. I don't know why. And the organisation's outreach to the ethnic communities wasn't very successful, probably because, when the ethnic communities have someone who is ill, they try to keep consultation and care in the community instead of looking for professional help. One interesting aspect was that my work with the association led me to conclude that the incidence of Alzheimer's, or indeed dementia in all of its forms, did not vary a great deal among different ethnic groups.

Trang's next move was to join the Board of the Australian Vietnam Women's Association, an organisation that, among its other activities, aims to find employment for Vietnamese migrant women through training and placement. Their methods of operation struck a chord with her, in particular those that focused on meeting aged-care needs.

> I think it is probably the most successful Vietnamese Association in

Australia, led by a group of formidable women. They ran a lot of projects and were able to get funding for them, as much as $2 million a year from various sources, including state and federal governments. They had about thirty professional staff and a really good CEO. And a good board. A lot of ethnic organisations rely on volunteers so their services might not be as effective or reliable. But this group attracted staff who stayed for many years. Many had been professionals back in Vietnam, including doctors, teachers and pharmacists. They looked for sources of employment for women. They provided services for the elderly in home care. And they ran a training program to help Vietnamese women to become aged-care workers. They had so many activities and for each they would apply for funding. So it was a very active and successful organisation.

Trang herself brought a great deal of expertise to the Association. A graduate of the Australian Institute of Company Directors (Dip. AICD) with years of service on the boards of public and private institutions, she was very experienced in corporate governance. She knew what could and should be done professionally and legally. 'And, although they were very good at preparing grant submissions,' she smiles, 'sometimes I might have had a connection.' Her involvement would continue until 2014, a substantial contribution to a special group.

While her family and friends were grateful for the extra time that Trang could devote to them after her retirement from RMIT, they were even happier that she was giving more priority to her own needs. Yet none of them really believed that the fires that drove her were significantly dampened. They were right. The following year, 2009, would see her maintain her professional efforts. She was still a director of the APS and by no means considered herself finished.

The year ended on a bright note with the birth of Zoe Trang, Elizabeth's second child. Trang also looked forward to a special event in mid-2010, the Congress of the International Association for Applied Psychology. Earlier in the decade, in her capacity as a director of the APS, she been a member of the committee set up to prepare Australia's bid to host the event. She and her colleagues had visited Singapore in 2004 to present the bid. She recalls the competitive process with clarity and humour:

The contending countries were Chile, South Africa and Australia. We were very well prepared, I think the best. We had PowerPoint presentations, which were still pretty new in those days, and the Australian Consulate hosted a cocktail reception for the selection committee and all attendees at the bidding session. The South African group was also very well prepared. And of course there was strong rivalry among the three bidders because the Congress was not often held in the Southern Hemisphere. Australia was a strong contender because of its political stability, quality institutions and facilities. But the negative point was that we were a very expensive country to visit, particularly for delegates from developing nations. And during the selection process we were grilled on our record on human rights because of both the controversy over our treatment of asylum seekers and our slow progress in bringing the living standards of our Indigenous peoples up to the national norm. It was really just a matter of luck that, at the time, I was an Assistant Human Rights Commissioner. I could answer the selection committee's questions with a good deal of authority, and that helped us a lot.

The occasion had its humorous side as well, although the South Africans might not have agreed. When the Australians had finished their presentation, they were standing near the entrance when their South Africans rivals arrived to make their case. They came with huge bags loaded with bottles of South African wine intended for the selection committee. Unfortunately, they mistook the Australians for the selection committee and presented them with the wine instead. In a double blow, the Aussies won the bid and returned triumphant with the wine.

After arriving back in Australia, Trang was appointed to the organising committee for the Congress, which she would address on the topic of her experiences in Australia as an overseas-born psychologist. She recalls the committee's preparations:

> The chosen venue was Melbourne's convention centre. Affordability was a dilemma for both the hosts and the attendees. Setting the registration fees too high would lessen the numbers coming from overseas, in particular from Third World countries, while reducing them too far

would lead to a deficit. The committee decided to charge the necessary rates to cover costs, but to offer free registration to some attendees from Third World countries as defined by the current UN classification table. But it wasn't as simple as that, of course. The plan just didn't work, because many prospective attendees from poorer countries couldn't afford the travel and accommodation costs. In the end there was only one person who was able to accept the offer of free registration.

It was while Trang and her colleagues were grappling with these matters that fate intervened to change the family life that was the source of so much happiness and contentment. David, the rock on which Trang relied so much, fell ill.

APS Director Trang. Photo taken by David for APS website, 2010.

- CHAPTER 40 -

Fateful Diagnosis

Melbourne, 2009

For some time David had not been well. He was experiencing breathlessness, tiring quickly after exertion. Climbing the stairs at home was becoming a problem. He duly consulted his doctor, who arranged for the necessary tests. The results made grim reading.

'It's not good news, David.' The specialist's face was a study in compassion, his words quiet and regretful. 'You are suffering from pulmonary fibrosis, in simple terms severe scarring of the lung tissue. There are many possible causes, some unidentifiable. So we might not be able to reach a firm conclusion on the specifics. But, whatever the cause, I have to tell you that it's a progressive condition for which we have no effective treatment. So your prognosis is very poor.'

David was visibly shocked, but as always thinking quickly. 'How long?'

'Statistically, about two years. Perhaps three. You're very unlucky, really. It's not a common condition. We can help you to stay comfortable during that time, of course.'

'And there is nothing at all to be done?'

The doctor looked away, gathering his thoughts. 'For a younger person, a lung transplant is the sole possibility. But I'm afraid that you don't fit the bill. There is already a waiting list for younger people, who are understandably given priority. I'm sorry, but that's the current policy. Fair but cruel, some would say.'

'What about extending the period? Is there nothing at all I can do?'

'Keep leading a healthy lifestyle. Try to walk for an hour a day to exercise your lungs. Concentrate on activities that you enjoy. That's about it.'

David thanked the specialist and left, still trying to come to terms with the diagnosis that had condemned him to a very different and all too brief future. His mind was already seething with plans, but first he had to break the news to Trang. She recalls her shock:

> I was shattered. There's just no other way to put it. After the initial shock, my thoughts turned to how I could best support him through his coming ordeal. He was at once angry and depressed, instinctively rejecting the reality that his life was to be cut so short. But he was ever the pragmatist as well. His first step was to resign from his appointments. Publicly, he did his best to carry on his normal life outside work. Privately, he began to put his affairs in order. It was imperative that he planned properly for my widowhood and for our daughters.
>
> Through all of this I was concerned too for his mental state in case his regrets should overwhelm him. I knew from my research into the aged just how corrosive that could be. As a counsellor, I knew also that David would benefit from psychological support. But now was not the time. He needed first to come fully to grips with the fact that his condition was terminal. Acceptance would make him more amenable to therapy. I felt so angry that the lung transplant option was closed to him because of his age. I was sure that was policy rather than the waiting list. They just said that no one did lung transplants at his age.

Even as she faced the inevitable, Trang knew that she too must maintain her commitments instead of spending each day trying vainly to ensure that David was comforted by her presence. Fussing over him would have the opposite effect. It was a difficult choice, but one that David supported wholeheartedly. He was bent on remaining positive. While his life had entered a new phase in which each month was torn painfully from the shrinking calendar of his existence, he gave little outward sign of his suffering. Rather, his public presentation made light of his illness. He was unfailingly a convivial host when their friends came to visit and, even as the passage of time reduced his physical abilities, the twinkling eyes and sunny smile reassured those close to him that it wasn't really happening, that somehow he would survive his illness. It was unthinkable that the man they knew and loved would have to haul down his flag to acknowledge the shadows that had enveloped him.

Given David's wish that she should maintain her professional activities, Trang continued to lead professional development tours abroad and showed by example the benefits of contributing actively on international platforms by joining the Australian bidding committee competing for selection as the host country of the 2020 International Congress of Psychology (ICP). She left the APS Board in 2011 after completing two five-year terms. She had given long service and believed it was time to make room for others who were keen to contribute. Reflecting on cultural change in the APS Board's operations during the preceding decade, she was pleased that the Society's proceedings now took place in a much more inclusive setting. In all, Trang had thoroughly enjoyed her time as a director and, for the moment, she was content that her diminishing workload allowed her much more time to spend with David and their grandchildren. Most importantly, she and David found a measure of relaxation and happiness in travel adventures with friends.

As always, however, there was more to do in the professional field. After her decision not to stand again for election to the APS Board, Trang still felt that she had more to offer. On 31 August 2012 she was appointed to the Psychology Board of Australia, the agency responsible for regulation of practitioner psychologists under the direction of the Australian Health Workforce Ministerial Council. The functions of the board include accreditation standards and registration of practitioners, together with the development of standards and codes for the profession. Its key role in the maintenance of rigorous practitioner requirements obliges all psychologists to ensure they are familiar with its registration standards, guidelines and code of ethics. Trang's three-year appointment to that board reflected the diversity of her experience with professional standards and development that she brought to the task.

David's condition and her continuing professional and community involvement aside, Trang's changing circumstances obviously involved a great deal of personal adjustment. There were more of her own health issues to address, until recently something she had only thought about in passing. Ever thorough, she joined a diabetes and diet research project. Given the extent of her travels to exotic locations, it was difficult at times to focus on what should be consumed rather than what alternatives were available. At the same time, her impending loss of David was ever in her thoughts. Then, in 2012, they had to sell their treasured home at Yarra Bank Court. David was no longer coping with climbing stairs, so a move to more suitable accommodation was necessary. Planning beyond that point was increasingly difficult. It would have been easy to slip into resentment and despair. Fortunately, there was a bright side to their lives. One of the particular rewards of their difficult years was the birth of a fourth grandchild. Helen and Sam's second child, Stephen, arrived in July 2011. The icing on the grandparental cake was that Stephen broke the run of granddaughters. Despite the ever-present reminders of David's decline, it would have been difficult to find prouder family elders. As Christmas 2012 loomed, they did their best to ignore the passing of time and find joy in the present.

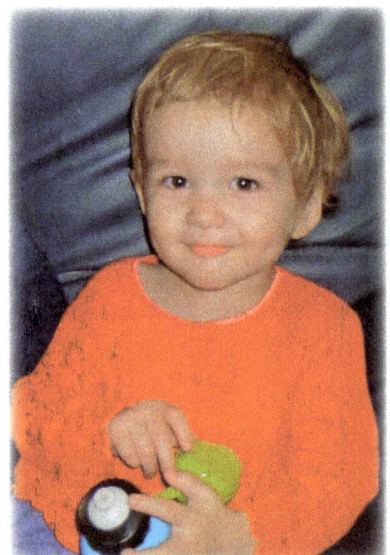

Grandson Stephen (Helen and Sam, 2011) broke the run of granddaughters. His elder sister Rebecca joined the family in 2008.

- CHAPTER 41 -

Troubled Times

Melbourne, 2012-14

After his expected two years and then three, David continued to battle his illness. Despite his courageous determination to not give in, the decline in his physical state was evident. Yet he continued to work through his bucket list, travelling with Trang whenever possible. He particularly enjoyed time spent in the north of Australia, including a Kimberley cruise and a Cape York safari. Visits to Europe, Fiji and South-East Asia rounded out his travel program. While at home, he continued to ensure his family's financial security through astute planning. On the weekends, he and Trang encouraged their friends to visit so their lives could at least maintain a sense of activity as usual.

Their family continued to grow, much to their joy. In 2012, Elizabeth and Dean produced their third daughter, Genevieve. But, all too soon, the dark clouds surrounded them again. Little more than a year later, with David still somehow pushing back the inevitable, Elizabeth was diagnosed with breast cancer. The news hit all of the family hard. There was a sense of disbelief that this insidious disease could strike the healthy young paediatrician and mother of three. Trang and David despaired. While David's illness had been a shock, at least they had known he was not well and he had been given time to prepare for his passing. With an aggressive cancer, there was no guarantee of any such period of grace for Elizabeth. She underwent painful chemotherapy for the following six months, remaining strong, insisting that her parents get on with their lives instead of giving up their activities to spend their time with her and the grandchildren. Ever conscious that her father's time was short, she wanted very much to spare him the mind-numbing experience of sitting around waiting for both of their situations to worsen. So Trang and David agreed reluctantly not to cancel activities they had already planned.

Several months earlier, David had told Trang that he felt ready to undergo counselling. She arranged regular sessions with a trusted colleague. While she kept at arm's length from the counselling, she was relieved that David was clearly responding well. He was becoming more and more accepting that, very soon, he would be unable to maintain even his limited activities. His last holiday was in early 2014, a visit to Cambodia and Vietnam with Trang and family members Kim, Chau and Kim Chi. The group included Trang's best friend, Lorraine Elliott, Lorraine's partner, John Kiely, and a group of APS psychologists.

It was a more relaxing cruise than Trang had expected, with ample activities on and off board, within an intriguing culture not so different from her own origins. David, too, enjoyed the journey. He joined each of the daily excursions, walking steadily with his group, returning to the ship in the afternoon to sit quietly with a beer or glass of wine as the setting sun bathed the river and its surrounds in the intense, ever-changing colours of early evening in the tropics. His dry humour and broad knowledge made him an engaging conversationalist, unfailingly good company over dinner and drinks. Then he would rest, husbanding his declining reserves of energy for the next day's activities. Best of all, good news came during the cruise. Elizabeth's chemotherapy had been successful, although there were still misgivings about the longer term.

In mid-February, Trang and David returned to Melbourne. He had weathered the journey well and they felt optimistic that his survival would continue into a fifth year. But that was not to be. His condition deteriorated quickly, to the extent that it could not be managed at home. He was hospitalised, but he and Trang remained hopeful that he would recover sufficiently to return home, even if only for a short while. In a cruel twist of fate, the policy that had prevented him from being placed on the waiting list for a lung transplant had been reversed in light of increasing life expectancies and the consequent expectation that working lives would become longer to help offset fiscal pressures of pensions and healthcare for the aged. Trang could not help but be angry:

The waiting time was only about six months. If he had been on the list from the beginning, he would have long since had the transplant. Now he was in hospital because his breathing had become so distressed, and the doctor said that he could be placed on the list. We thought that he would come out again and that he had the chance to survive until his name came up. But that was not to be. By late April, it became evident that palliative care was the only option. His psychologist supported him to the end, which came just weeks later, on 17 May. After he died, she told me he had been at peace, that he had accepted his end and that I must take comfort from that acceptance.

It was good advice, Trang knew. But like so much good advice, it would not be easy to follow. In the meantime, there were arrangements to make and other pressing concerns to address. And, for the first time in more than four decades, she spent time alone in her home. Everywhere she looked she was reminded of David's companionable presence and his readiness to act as a sounding board for her ideas and plans. Mother's advice to her daughters so long ago came into her mind. 'You must study hard and learn to become independent,' she would tell them. 'Remember that you must also plan to be a widow.' Even more sound advice, she thought wryly, but widowhood brought grief and intense loneliness as well. Mother hadn't mentioned that.

Happy family, 2013. Trang, flanked by David with Rebecca and Helen with Stephen, holds Elizabeth's third daughter Genevieve, the fifth grandchild. At the rear, first grandchild Evie and father Dean look on while Elizabeth (centre) holds second daughter Zoe.

- CHAPTER 42 -

Vale David

Melbourne, May-July 2014

The chapel was crowded. The large gathering of colleagues, politicians, family and friends from every period of David's life spilled from the doorway into the venue's surrounds. Each mourner clutched a copy of the Order of Service, that final marker of a life completed. *Celebration of the Life of David John Thomas, 29 January 1945-17 May 2014*. Not a long life by today's expectations, but long enough to give forty-five years to his marriage and family. Trang sat quietly, smiling gently in response to condolences as she reflected one more time on their lives together, concentrating deeply on the positives because she was only just holding it together. She listened intently while David's eulogists, lifelong friend Richard Deane-Butcher and former political protégée Paula Davey, traced his journey of high achievement and reminded those present of just how much this man had given of himself so that others might succeed. They spoke also of his enduring relationship with Trang and his huge love for his greatest of legacies, his daughters and grandchildren. Too quickly it was Trang's turn to put her feelings into words.

She could not speak for long, because there was too much to say. But she managed a smile and even flashes of nostalgic humour as she paid tribute to David as the generous, loving and supportive life partner he had been:

> David my love. Thank you for forty-five years of being together, of being my friend, soulmate, partner and mentor. When we married, many people were surprised. Your ex- girlfriends were all tall, slim, blond, speaking perfect English, everything that I was not. Some said 'What a waste of a tall guy.' My friends said you were too shy and introverted, refusing to dance, refusing to flirt. Your father was doubtful,

my father was furious. They all said it wouldn't last. But we survived. Of course, we were very different. You loved your wine and I am allergic to alcohol. You always had to finish a full bottle by yourself because I could not share it with you. You loved buying lottery tickets but, me being Buddhist, I do not believe in getting something for nothing. Of course there were difficult times. The time we were so poor when Elizabeth was born, three of us living on your postgraduate scholarship. But we progressed to the time when we had enough money so you could make sure that the children could do whatever they needed to do. And along the way there were so many happy times that I cannot recount. I will never know another person with a brilliant mind like yours, a supporter whose judgement I absolutely trusted. All of these years I have relied so much on you. Every journal article that I wrote, every grant application, every speech that I made must first be read by you. You read every draft of my PhD thesis, commented on all of my job applications and advised me on my actions at work. You were truly the wind beneath my wings.

David, you will live on through our beautiful grandchildren. Some have already shown superior skills in reading, in language, that must have come from you. I am frightened of living without you, without your guidance, and I will miss you forever. Thank you. I love you.

Among those present at David's service were Trang's best friend, Lorraine. She was very ill, exhausted from treatment for a recurrence of breast cancer that had been detected soon after their return from the Mekong cruise a few months earlier. This time she did not respond to therapy, succumbing to her illness only a few weeks later. Trang, still grappling with the loss of David, was immensely saddened by Lorraine's passing. Their relationship, which had begun when Lorraine welcomed her to the Liberal women's group twenty-five years earlier, had steadily strengthened over the years since. During an interview on the Mekong cruise, Lorraine had been forthcoming about their shared interests and experiences:

> We met through politics, but with us it's more the friendship thing. I think the glue that binds you together when you are with other people

is knowing that you can relax, that you don't have to watch what you're saying all the time. Our friendship is like that. Shared beliefs and activities create bonds. Like the walking group that we started. It grew from a couple of us going for regular walks to become this eclectic Saturday-morning group. Some of them don't see each other at any other time. They just turn up on Saturday mornings. All sorts of backgrounds, including one man who is a refugee from the Exclusive Brethren. It's just a funny group. Of course they don't all come every Saturday. You have to be at the fountain in Albert Street at nine o'clock or we leave without you. We have a nice breakfast afterwards. And Trang has another wonderful gift. Everyone will be talking and then there will be a gap in the conversation and Trang will drop in an absolute pearl. She just has a wonderful sense of timing.

Once a year the walking women have a dinner and of course we're a mixed lot so there are differing culinary needs and cultural norms. But it has worked out very well. It's just another example of the group, which comfortably crosses both political and religious boundaries. There is no need for reserve. We spent a lot of time talking about weight and Trang dieting for Helen's wedding to fit into her costume. So in that way she displays that humorous element that is very much a part of your typical Australian.

There are other sides to Trang that I admire. Family is the bedrock. You can see with her sisters on this trip that family means so much to her. And she is so generous, to both her family and others. For example, my daughter had her first child later in life. Caroline was over forty and Trang had an afternoon tea for her to bring the baby along. I was very touched by that. In so many ways, I know that my life would be the poorer if I didn't know Trang, if I'd never known her.

Lorraine's tribute is a strong reminder that Trang, no matter how busy her life, is not one to forget her friends. There were the mothers who joined her playgroup when she was first a suburban housewife, with Elizabeth on her hip and no friends in the locality. Then her APS colleagues and the friends she had made on the many boards, councils and committees she served upon.

And, not least, the enduring friendships born of both her representative and private travels. None is left behind or forgotten. There is no doubt she has had her detractors and enemies as well. In Australia, assertive tall poppies are not always well regarded. However, as David was wont to say, 'If you have no enemies, it is difficult to appreciate fully your friends.' As she embarked on her widowhood, Trang's ability to maintain loyal friendships would stand her in good stead.

- CHAPTER 43 -

Widow Trang

Aboard the *Celebrity Constellation*, Mediterranean Sea, September 2016

Trang was among the handful of early risers who exercised at the cruise liner's well-equipped gymnasium before breakfast each morning. Located above and behind the soaring structure of the bridge, the gym provided a panoramic view of sea and land during the ship's stately approach to the port of the day. It had been a most engaging week since departing from Venice – sunny days of excursions in Italy, Slovenia, Croatia and Montenegro, then time to relax during the longer stage into the Mediterranean to visit Malta. The ship would backtrack to Sicily before disembarking her passengers at Civitavecchia to spend time in Rome. The early spring weather was superb, the sea a calm lake that barely registered the *Constellation's* passage.

She stood watching Malta rise slowly above the horizon, sliding towards her as if eager to welcome this next wave of visitors. As always, she reflected on her many previous journeys and the joy she had always felt when David had shared them. Two years of widowhood had helped her to accept his loss, and she was grateful for the comfort she had taken from the support of friends and colleagues during the professional development tours she had continued to lead. This would be the last, but her love of travel would never be extinguished.

It was time, she decided, to bring her story up to date.

Melbourne, 2015

Trang smiles gently as she describes life without David, nostalgia overlaid with wry acceptance.

> I still battle grief and depressed mood, but I have had time to consider and deal with most of the impacts on my life. I miss his old-fashioned gentlemanly responses, the way he always opened doors for me and stood up when I came into the room. I miss his love and companionship and there are constant reminders of how much I treasured and relied upon his wisdom and his caring support. He was truly the man behind the woman, my trusted consultant in complex or difficult situations. We were a good team, you see, and when half of a good team is lost then the surviving partner has to reshape so much of what was an established, mutually rewarding way of life. Suddenly you are alone on the tiny island that you shared for so long.

It is typical of Trang's Buddhist calm and pragmatism that, while she acknowledges the lost dimension of shared goals and activities, she also emphasises the positive aspects of reshaping her life. Fortunately, she deals well with change. After five decades crowded with work, collaboration and achievement, time on her own has brought the freedom of making decisions for herself and being able to act on impulse. She is content to go unaccompanied to the opera or the ballet or a movie, something she would not have done without checking David's plans first. Her daily routine, other than time set aside for work and childminding, is now determined by her freedom to go wherever her mood takes her.

Work is now far less demanding, of course. Following David's loss, Trang completed her three-year appointment to the Psychology Board of Australia and also served on Victoria's Mental Health Tribunal. Still a member of the APS, she maintains a professional involvement that sits comfortably with her other life obligations and interests.

She is surprised to find that she is really enjoying female rather than male company now, a reflection perhaps of her move away from male-dominated environments:

> I belong to various clubs, including the Lyceum and the Vietnamese Women's Club. And I choose female doctors, lawyers and whatever other professionals I need. Why? Because even now I feel that men treat me differently. All too often there's still that hint of patronising behaviour. But with women I can be both friend and client. I'm still

learning a lot of the financial stuff, of course, because David always handled our finances. But I really enjoy working with these women.

Another positive is that Trang, ever a caring and generous woman, can now afford to give way more freely to her philanthropic urges. There is a hint of mischief in her smile as she lists some of her causes:

My widowhood enables me to give away some of the money David left me. I don't need it all, so in my own small way I like to contribute to others. I asked the girls to name their favourite charities so that I could make donations. Helen nominated the St Kilda Mums, an organisation that helps disadvantaged mothers with comparatively expensive baby needs such as prams, cots and clothes. Elizabeth nominated the Peter MacCallum Cancer Research Foundation.

Then there is the Buddhist Society of Victoria. I go there regularly for meditation. They have a project going, to build a monastery in the forest outside Melbourne. They bought an old farmhouse and they are doing a lot of fundraising. There is a list of things to be done, one of which is to ensure that the women's quarters are properly heated. So I asked them to let me fund that particular project. 'Fix it straight away,' I said, so they will have the warmth next winter. So these are some of the ways in which I am spending David's money. And I can do it without having to ask him. It's strange, I know, but having extra money is in some ways a burden to me. I don't want to be preoccupied with decisions about where to invest, how best to manage the money.

While I am coping well with change, it takes longer for the emotional side to adjust. I started taking a lot of videos of David during that last year, in particular when he was with the grandchildren, playing with them, laughing with them. I still have the videos on my computer, but I can't yet bear to look at them. I will when I am ready. And the kids will love them too.

Her expression portrays much more effectively than words the solace Trang has found in helping to care for her grandchildren. 'I feel so lucky,' she says. 'Each week, for two or three days they come to my place and I look after them. They fill up my days.'

It is tempting to close this account of Trang's life and times with this happy picture of her ongoing involvement in philanthropic activity and family, a fulfilling life stretching into a joyful retirement. But her story is far from ended. For all of her newfound freedom of choice, she once more found herself living in the shadow of an even greater threat to her happiness. As if to remind her that fate often visits further hardship on those who have known grief, by 2015 Elizabeth was again grappling with her life-threatening condition. The cancer she had fought so well two years earlier had returned. It was inoperable and she was again undergoing prolonged, painful treatment.

The entire family was once again traumatised. Trang, ever the professional problem-solver, found it hugely difficult to cope with her feelings of helplessness. 'Elizabeth is so young,' she said sadly. 'Three young children and so much of her life and career to come. I can help them financially, give them whatever they need, but that's poor consolation. I am so anxious.'

She sought to address her anxiety and depressed mood by attending meditation classes each night Monday to Thursday at the Buddhist Centre. She describes the comfort that meditation brings:

> It is just so calming. People like me come in and there is guidance and when it is finished we leave again. There is no social activity, and that's good because social activity is not what I need. The meditation classes help me to cope but it is so difficult. I sit down and try to focus but my mind is still running off in many directions. I have so much yet to learn about dealing with life's way of reminding us how little can be taken for granted, no matter how well we plan. There is no logic in it. I cannot use my tried and trusted research methods to gain insight and understanding. I just have to accept that all that can be done is being done. I think it is the biggest challenge of my life. I coped when Mother died. David's passing was a huge loss, but again I coped. I was very upset when my father died because of the circumstances that led to his death. If he had been able to stay in Vietnam his life would have been much longer and happier. But the war, their flight and Mother's illness along the way - it was all just too much for him. And then we

lost Quynh to the re-education camp and Kim's children to the sea. I somehow coped with all of that. But this is different.

Paradoxically, it was Elizabeth who comforted Trang:

> She remained so cheerful and optimistic, still making her plans to do this and to do that. As if she intended to live to a hundred. I actually felt better when I was with her. She was so strong, so brave. I suggested that she think about doing some relaxation and meditation classes, but instead she found strength in her strong religious beliefs and the circle of close friends in her church group. They provided constant encouragement and support. That was her way of coping and sharing. Her very close friend Judy is a minister and loving supporter. That was a blessing. Even so, and, although I loved having the children, I wished so much that I could do more.

In these circumstances, Trang was reluctant to leave home for even short periods. Elizabeth, knowing that her mother needed the distractions of work and occasional travel, insisted that she stick to her plans for travel and continuing engagement with the APS. She duly attended the fiftieth anniversary of the establishment of the APS in September 2015. Once more, but hopefully not for the last time, Trang took her place behind the lectern in response to yet another fine gesture of recognition from her peers.

- CHAPTER 44 -

Recognition, Reprieve and Continuing Challenge

2015-16

Trang was very proud to have received the 2014 APS President's Award for Distinguished Contribution to Psychology in Australia. Coincidentally, the foundation of the APS and Trang's arrival in the country that was to become her home both took place in the mid-1960s. More than any other symbol of her achievements, the award, presented at the APS fiftieth anniversary conference, recognised both her long history of constructive participation in her profession and her distinguished record of service to the Australian community. Her citation lists her many roles and achievements, concluding with the statement that 'Emeritus Professor Thomas's work record reflects extraordinary depth and breadth, and represents the career of a fine academic, scholar and teacher as well as a model of a compassionate woman bringing her considerable psychological expertise to bear on the wider society.'

Trang listened quietly as APS President Professor Michael Kyrios traced her story, commencing with her early life in Vietnam and outlining her remarkable achievements since beginning her tertiary education at UNSW in 1965. He added his personal views about the qualities that enabled Trang to rise to unforeseen heights:

> My only regret about this award is that it wasn't awarded by me. My predecessor got in first. But I am proud to be here today. Trang has always been a supporter and a role model for me. She became the go-to person in Asian multiculturalism. And that's a term I'd like to bring back. It was in an age when we needed leaders among women in academic and community affairs. She was a natural for so many community affairs appointments and received many awards for her work.

Knowing Trang as I do, it would be an enormous oversight not to mention her values. She is an amazing mother and grandmother who is still very much in caring roles. I know her daughter Elizabeth, who became a doctor, because my wife and I had the pleasure of teaching her at Melbourne University. And her daughter Helen, who also completed an honours degree and is an extraordinary musician. Having taught Elizabeth, I have had a first-hand account of the enormous influence for good that Trang has had on her family and on women in her sphere.

Trang, and of course David, have been an incredibly generous and giving couple. To observe Trang's ability to accept adversity and turn it into generosity is to see what resilience really means. And Trang has experienced more than her fair share of challenges, in particular those arising from the tragic circumstances of her family's struggle to escape from Vietnam in the aftermath of war. Through all of these ordeals, Trang supported her family by every means available to her. She showed true guts, resolve, passion and loyalty at every step of the way. And while the challenges of life continue, Trang continues to give and give, never looking to receive.

It is my great pleasure to present this award to a woman who represents the strength of character, the ethical and social standing, the highest degree of accomplishment, the highest of community and family values and the best of what psychology has to offer to the world.

Trang responded to these words of praise with her accustomed poise and humility. But her listeners were aware of the fear for Elizabeth and her family that stalked her every waking moment. Her feeling of helplessness persisted as she returned to Melbourne to combine her supporting role with continuing prayer and meditation. Despite her faith, when the breakthrough came she could scarcely believe the good news. After long and painful months of chemotherapy and immunotherapy at the Peter MacCallum Cancer Centre, progress tests had shown that Elizabeth's condition had improved. However, it would a long, stressful wait until further tests in February 2016 could confirm that her aggressive tumour had continued to retreat. When it came, the news was again positive. Elizabeth would be able to cease chemotherapy and continue with her immunological treatment. Buoyed by this result, Trang dared to hope that her daughter's strength and faith had finally prevailed. Sadly, at the time of writing, the cancer has returned yet again and Elizabeth is undergoing the latest and best available treatment. As always, she remains unbowed and unbeaten.

It is most difficult to end this account of Trang's life of achievement on this inconclusive note. She bears her constant anxiety with stoicism, giving unstintingly of her resources and prayer in support of her family. Hope burns brightly in her, but there is only one element of certainty in her future. Trang is Trang, a truly indomitable woman. Whatever challenges she faces, her life will surely continue to reflect the values and ideals of Mother, that outstanding role model whose views and leadership shaped her family's world. Mother had much to be proud of in all of her children's achievements. No doubt she would have been doubly pleased and proud had she lived to witness the full extent of her youngest daughter's affirmation that 'the more you give, the more you will receive'.

- Acknowledgements -

It has taken me several years to fit this story into my life, and my obsessive nature (there's insight for you!) has no doubt played its part. Thank you to my wife, Robyn, and all of my friends and fellow travellers who encouraged me to undertake this happy venture. To Trang and her family members, colleagues and friends who kindly agreed to be interviewed, in locations as far flung as the Mekong River, Mumbai and the Mediterranean, my appreciation for your enthusiasm and anecdotal input. Sharing your collective knowledge and memories has been my great pleasure as well as adding an extra dimension to our travel experiences. I miss very much my conversations with Trang's late husband, David, in the afterglow of a glass or two and the beauty of sunset over the Mekong.

Special thanks to Sir James Gobbo AC CVO QC, eminent jurist and former Governor of Victoria, for contributing the Foreword. Your words reflect your appreciation for the full extent of Trang's service to the Australian community and her commitment to fairness and equal opportunity in an increasingly multicultural society.

Every book needs an editor, and I thank Trang's daughter, Helen, for referring me to her colleague Kerry Davies. I learned much from Kerry about structure, consistency and when not to use semi-colons. She also encouraged me to highlight Trang's enduring love of travel and its relevance to my research. This work has indeed been a journey in more ways than one.

Finally, but not least, bouquets to Michelle Holyhead of The Book Studio for her skills and creativity in book design. Well done, Michelle, and may your studio continue to flourish.

www.ingramcontent.com/pod-product-compliance
Lightning Source LLC
Chambersburg PA
CBHW062057290426
44110CB00022B/2620